Table of Contents

Introduction

Security makes all else possible, to include governance, economic growth, and social well-being. Police provide that security for the people and the state, serving, in one analyst's words, "as the cornerstone of host nation security forces."[1] Yet, in many failing and failed states, the police need considerable assistance to develop into a force capable of providing security. Former Secretary of Defense Robert Gates addressed the necessity of developing partner capacity through a "whole of government" approach in a 2010 article entitled "Helping Others Defend Themselves." He wrote that the department-level agencies – particularly the Department of State (DOS), the Department of Justice (DOJ), and the Department of Defense (DOD) – could collectively "help other countries better provide for their own security [which] will be a key and enduring test of America's global leadership and a critical part of protecting national security, as well."[2]

By building partner capacity and fostering security abroad, through security sector reform (SSR), stability operations (SO), and security force assistance (SFA), the United States Government (USG) will in turn increase security at home.[3] The draw-down of forces in Iraq and Afghanistan provides the USG the opportunity to prioritize SSR, SO, and the development of partner capacity as prescribed by the 2010 National Security Strategy, the 2010 Quadrennial Diplomacy and Development Review, the 2010 Quadrennial Defense Review, the Army

---

[1] Beth Cole, ed. *Guiding Principles for Stabilization and Reconstruction* (Washington, DC: USIP Press, 2009), 17; "Civil Power in Irregular Conflict," Peacekeeping and Stability Operations Institute, http://pksoi.army mil/PKM/publications/reports/documents/CNA_PKSOI_civil-power-in-irregular-conflict_all.pdf.

[2] Robert Gates, "Helping Others Defend Themselves," http://www.foreignaffairs.com/articles/66224/robert-m-gates/helping-others-defend-themselves.

[3] Ted Strickler, "What the QDDR Says about Interagency Coordination," *InterAgency Journal* 2, no. 1 (Winter 2011): 67; Thorsten Stodiek, "OSCE's Police-Related Activities: Lessons Learned During the Last Decade," *Security and Human Rights*, no. 3 (2009): 201.

Capstone Concept, and recently revised Army doctrine.[4] These capstone documents call on the agencies to conduct SSR and build partner capacity to prevent states from failing or to re-establish the security apparatus and governance of failed states in order to enhance the security of the global community, especially the United States.[5]

With 2014 on the horizon, the USG must find a way to organize, plan, and develop a comprehensive SSR program, especially for host nation police advisory (HNPA) missions.[6] One mission will not succeed without the other; SSR requires a holistic HNPA approach, relying on an equitably developed security triad: police, justice, and corrections. HNPA missions form a critical sub-component of SSR and therefore support the overarching National Security Strategy.[7] While both missions require significant reforms in order to enable the USG to build partner capacity and improve security in failing or failed states, the following analysis seeks to demonstrate how DOD,

---

[4] "National Security Strategy," White House, http://www.whitehouse.gov/sites/default/files/rss_viewer/national_security_strategy.pdf; "Quadrennial Diplomacy and Development Review," Department of State, http://www.state.gov/documents/organization/153142.pdf; "Quadrennial Defense Review," Department of Defense, http://www.defense.gov/qdr/images/QDR_as_of_12Feb10_1000.pdf; "The Army Capstone Concept," US Army TRADOC, http://www.tradoc.army mil/tpubs/pams/tp525-3-0.pdf; U.S. Army, "Field Manual 3-07, Stability Operations," (Washington, DC: Headquarters, Department of the Army, October 2008); ———, "Field Manual 3-07.1, Security Force Assistance," (Washington, DC: Headquarters, Department of the Army, May 2009); ———, "ATTP 3-39.10 (FM 19-10), Law and Order Operations," (Washington, DC: Headquarters, Department of the Army, June 2011).

[5] Robert Caslen, "Change 1 to Field Manual 3-0 The Way the Army Fights Today," *Military Review* (March-April 2011): 87; William Caldwell and Steven Leonard, "Field Manual 3-07, Stability Operations: Upshifting the Engine of Change," *Military Review* (July-August 2008): 58.

[6] Nicholas Riegg, "Concepts and Systems for States in Crisis," *InterAgency Journal* 1, no. 1 (Fall 2010): 38, 40; "ICITAP Strategic Plan Fiscal Years 2009-2013," Department of Justice: Criminal Division, http://www.justice.gov/criminal/icitap/about/strategic-plan html.

[7] Although Both Bayley and Perito introduce the concept of the security triad in which the triad reflects the police, the judicial and the correction apparti of the state, for the purposes of this paper the term security triad has been expanded. Security triad for the purposes of this monograph reflects:that eestablishing ROL requires prioritizing the synchronized and integrated development of police, justice, and prison systems that are legitimate in both the eyes of the people and the international community. David Bayley and Robert Perito, *The Police in War: Sighting Insurgency, Terrorism, and Violent Crime* (Boulder, CO: Lynne Rienner Publishers, Inc, 2010), 39; Robert Perito, *Where is the Lone Ranger When We Need Him? America's Search for a Postconflict Stability Force* (Washington, DC: United States Institute of Peace Press, 2004), 328; FM 3-07 shows how HNPA nests in SFA, the military component of SSR. DOD conducts SFA in support of DOS's SSR mission.U.S. Army, "Field Manual 3-07, Stability Operations," 6-1 thru 6-3.

through the United States Army Military Police Corps, can assist the execution of HNPA missions more effectively. [8]

Background

United States department-level agencies have a long history of conducting missions to build partner capacity and providing HNPA support around the world.[9] As early as 1898, America conducted peace operations through a constabulary force, securing Cuba, during the Spanish-American War. The agencies, specifically the War Department and the Department of State also conducted highly effective constabulary missions after both WWI and WWII.[10] Later, in 1954, as combat operations in the Korean War ended and the Cold War continued, the USG established the Public Administration Board, in order to conduct what doctrine now refers to as SSR, SO, and SFA. The Public Administration Board sought to eliminate the spread of Communism, foster democracy and the rule of law (ROL), and safeguard American interests and ideals. [11]

The USG established the Public Administration Board, later renamed the Office of Public Safety (OPS), to conduct SSR, specifically HNPA with the appropriate authorities and lines of funding. For over twenty years, the organization supported containment by bolstering failing states and preventing the spread of communism, while providing technical advice, training, and

---

[8] The integration and participation of the MP Corps within the greater HNPA mission not only enhances the USG's performance, but also to saves money by streamlining the processes, encouraging interagency cooperation, and reducing duplication. David Glaser, Email correspondence with author. Provided insight and commentary regarding content of monograph, February 9, 2012.

[9] Perito, *Where is the Lone Ranger When We Need Him? America's Search for a Postconflict Stability Force*: 3.

[10] "Host Nation Policing Advising Training Support Package: Police Advising Overview," (Fort Leonard Wood, MO: United States Army Military Police School, 2011), Slides 5-7.

[11] Reg Davis and Harry James, "The Public Safety Story," in *The Public Safety Newsletter* (Santee, CA2001); Nadia Gerspacher, "The History of International Police Cooperation: A 150-year Evolution in Trends and Approaches," *Global Crime* 9, no. 1-2 (February-May 2008): 174; Elizabeth Hume and Michael Miklaucic, "Exorcising Demons of the Past: Seizing New Opportunities to Promote Democratic Policing," in *2005 USAID Summer Seminar Series* (USAID, July 7, 2005).

resources for civilian and paramilitary police. OPS not only worked abroad but also established the International Police Academy in 1963 in Washington, DC, to promote international standards and to train police officers in the methods necessary for an effective police force.[12] Such training emphasized, "professional and transparent law enforcement institutions that protect human rights, combat corruption, and reduce the threat of transnational crime and terrorism," and this philosophy remains the focus of the HNPA mission.[13]

The International Police Academy not only instructed police officers from the international community, but also helped to create a network of police organizations and foster partnership amongst many nations. Unfortunately, in 1974 allegations of program mismanagement and reports of human rights abuse within partner nations forced Congress to cancel funding for OPS and prohibited the training of foreign police.[14]

By the conclusion of the Cold War twenty-four years later, America again realized the importance of HNPA to regional security and sought ways to bolster failing and failed states through training of their security apparatuses. Subsequently, in support of our national interests the government empowered various agencies to conduct HNPA on a case-by-case basis.[15] For example, DOS, DOJ, and DOD worked together to conduct SSR and HNPA in Panama, Kosovo, and Haiti. However, due to their ad hoc nature, the success of these missions varied greatly, as did the method of planning, organization, execution, and assessment.

---

[12] Walter Ladwig, "Training Foreign Police: A Missing Aspect of U.S Security Assistance to Counterinsurgency," *Comparative Strategy: An International Journal* 26, no. 4 (July-September 2007): 288.

[13] Davis and James, "The Public Safety Story," 5-6, 15, 27; U.S. Department of Justice, "About ICITAP," http://www.justice.gov/criminal/icitap/.

[14] Davis and James, "The Public Safety Story," 3-8; Ladwig, "Training Foreign Police: A Missing Aspect of U.S Security Assistance to Counterinsurgency," 288-89.

[15] "Host Nation Policing Advising Training Support Package: Police Advising Overview."; Robert Perito, "U.S. Police in Peace and Stability Operations," United States Institute of Peace Press, www.usip.org; Bayley and Perito, *The Police in War: Sighting Insurgency, Terrorism, and Violent Crime*: 119.

The Foreign Assistance Act (FAA) of 1974, Section 660, prohibits United States agencies from engaging with foreign law enforcement agencies. However, Congress has long recognized the "need for assistance programs to 'help develop institutions with the administration of justice'" on a case-by-case basis.[16] Thus, America continued to engage with foreign institutions including police organizations, justice departments, and the corrections system, conducting ad hoc SSR and HNPA programs. [17] In 2011, the USG Accountability Office (GAO) reported that funding for seven agencies and twenty-four components to conduct or facilitate HNPA totaled more than $3.5 billion dollars in 2009 alone. This funding level illustrates the growing emphasis on HNPA missions. For example, in 1990 America spent only$180 million dollars on HNPA missions worldwide.[18] Unfortunately, the USG increase in funding did not correlate to an increase in coordination amongst the department-level agencies or an increase in the development of an overarching program.[19]

Over twenty-four USG organizations play a role in SSR and HNPA. However, only a few agencies focus their efforts on such missions. These organizations include the DOJ's Office of Prosecutorial Development Assistance and Training (OPDAT) and International Criminal Investigative Training Assistance Program (ICITAP); the DOS's International Narcotics and Law Enforcement Affairs Office (INL); the Office of the Coordinator for Reconstruction and

---

[16] "Host Nation Policing Advising Training Support Package: Police Advising Overview."; "Foreign Assistance Meeting the Training Needs of Police in New Democracies," Government Accountability Office, http://www.gao.gov/products/NSIAD-93-109; Ladwig, "Training Foreign Police: A Missing Aspect of U.S Security Assistance to Counterinsurgency," 289.

[17] Hume and Miklaucic, "Exorcising Demons of the Past: Seizing New Opportunities to Promote Democratic Policing," notes.

[18] Joseph Christoff, "U.S. Agencies Provided Billions of Dollars to Train and Equip Foreign Police Forces," U.S. Government Accountability Officce, http://www.gao.gov/multimedia/podcasts/581557; "Multiple U.S. Agencies Provided Billions of Dollars to Train and Equip Foreign Police Forces," US Government Accountability Office, http://www.gao.gov/products/GAO-11-402R.

[19] "Multiple U.S. Agencies Provided Billions of Dollars to Train and Equip Foreign Police Forces," (Washington, DC: Government Accountability Office, April 2011), 16; ———, "Training and Equipping Foreign Police Forces," General Accounting Office, www.gao.gov/podcast/watchdog_episode_56 html; Ladwig, "Training Foreign Police: A Missing Aspect of U.S Security Assistance to Counterinsurgency," 292.

Stabilization (S/CRS); and the United States Agency for International Development (USAID).[20] All of these organizations should habitually collaborate with DOD military elements, to include the United States Army Military Police (MP) Corps, in order to conduct and fund HNPA missions. Although these organizations cooperated for over twenty years to accomplish missions in South and Central America, the Balkans, and in Iraq and Afghanistan, their efforts remain disjointed and redundant.[21] This results primarily from a lack of interagency doctrine and unclear lines of authority and funding. Specifically, the agencies lack proper authorities and national strategy to guide the execution of SSR and HNPA resulting in poorly defined objectives and no long-term strategy.[22] Additionally, because no lead agency coordinates the efforts of various organizations conducting of HNPA missions, their execution suffers from the lack of institutional knowledge, doctrine, or even a common lexicon. Furthermore, the absence of a lead agency results in a lack of transparency and accountability. Finally, HNPA missions suffer from unpredictable funding availability as the USG struggles through annual budget shortages, exacerbated by the changes in national strategy caused by periodic elections. Both issues impede effective strategy development and overall mission effectiveness, resulting in chronic under resourcing, ad hoc organization and command and control structures, and a lack of agreement on mission requirements and objectives.[23]

---

[20] "Multiple U.S. Agencies Provided Billions of Dollars to Train and Equip Foreign Police Forces"; "Office of Overseas Prosecutorial Development, Assistance and Training," U.S. Department of Justice, http://www.justice.gov/criminal/opdat/; " International Criminal Investigative Training Assistance Program," U.S. Department of Justice, http://www.justice.gov/criminal/icitap/; "Bureau of International Narcotics and Law Enforcement Affairs," U.S. Department of State, http://www.state.gov/g/inl/; "Bureau of Conflict and Stabilization Operations," U.S. Department of State, http://www.state.gov/j/cso/; "U.S. Agency for International Development," U.S. Agency for International Development, http://www.usaid.gov/.

[21] Perito, *Where is the Lone Ranger When We Need Him? America's Search for a Postconflict Stability Force*: Introduction.

[22] Stodiek, "OSCE's Police-Related Activities: Lessons Learned During the Last Decade," 204.

[23] Due to the USG's overall ineffective planning and execution of HNPA, the MP Corps must serve as a stopgap, capable of integrated planning and initial execution of HNPA until greater USG resources are allocated and integrated. Glaser. John Martin, "Training Indigenous Security Forces at the

While the various USG agencies seek to facilitate HNPA missions abroad, the USG

currently lacks the force structure to conduct SSR and HNPA effectively. Because no single

organization leads the planning and execution of HNPA missions at the national level, each

individual agency often resorts to hiring contractors to staff and facilitate the mission. However,

this leads to a costly and slow method of conducting HNPA that suffers from limited capacity and

inconsistent execution.[24] Therefore, the DOD routinely serves as the force provider post conflict,

charged with supporting and at times executing HNPA missions, even though it does not possess

the best-suited force for executing HNPA missions. Most military personnel receive little or no

HNPA-specific training. Even MPs, trained in escalation of force and the interpersonal skills

required to deal with the public, lack the depth of expertise to partner at all levels, from local to

national, and within some specific field of police work. MPs lack manpower depth and the

training and education framework to develop the required institutional support and sustainment

mechanisms within host nation (HN) governments to ensure the long-term viability of the

mission.[25]

Personnel providing HNPA seek to institute policing reforms, built around the concept of

community based policing.[26] However, military personnel – even MPs – tend to mold the HN

Upper End of the Counterinsurgency Spectrum," *Military Review* 86, no. 6 (November/December 2006): 62; "U.S. Security," Global Security, http://www.globalsecurity.org/intell/library/reports/gao/920300-train.htm.

[24] Perito, *Where is the Lone Ranger When We Need Him? America's Search for a Postconflict Stability Force*: 328; Strickler, "What the QDDR Says about Interagency Coordination," 73; "U.S. Security".

[25] There are specific elements and components within the Military Police Corps that provide expertise, which rivals other USG assets, especially in a deployed environment. For example, the Criminal Investigation Command (CID) specialists who facilitate training and mentorship in fraud, digital forensics, and cyber crimes. "Host Nation Policing Advising Training Support Package: Police Advising Overview."; Martin, "Training Indigenous Security Forces at the Upper End of the Counterinsurgency Spectrum," 61; Ben Fitzgerald and Scott Brady, "Considerations for the Employment of Transitional Law Enforcement Capabilities," Peacekeeping and Stability Operations Institute, http://pksoi.army mil/PKM/documents/Noetic%20TLE%20Project%20Considerations%20for%20TLE%20-%20Jan%2009.pdf.

[26] USAID defines community based policing as "the partnership between the police and the community work on specific solutions to specific problems. This approach focuses on service to the

police in their own image.[27] Police should not act like or function as a military force; rather, police should serve as a force receptive to and supportive of the people.[28] They should focus on internal, not external, security. However, with appropriate coordination and pre-execution planning, police experts from various government agencies, trained on the HN's legal system and the cultural complexities of the region, could augment DOD forces to overcome the limitations of MP units. These experts would provide the critical experience and technical expertise required to develop a police force in its entirety, complimenting DOD's tactical level efforts and the DOS's and DOJ's judicial and corrections efforts, in order to establish ROL. Thus, the USG would prioritize the synchronized and integrated development of police, justice, and prison systems that are legitimate in both the eyes of the people and the international community. Therefore, a whole of government approach could improve the effectiveness of USG HNPA missions, but this will require extensive reforms so the USG can achieve unity of effort.[29]

---

community and views police as problem solvers and community advocates...Community policing emphasizes community engagement, organizational transformation, and working with citizens to solve problems which requiers officers to think independently and to be able to makes deicisions on their own in order to best serve the community. Hume and Miklaucic, "Exorcising Demons of the Past: Seizing New Opportunities to Promote Democratic Policing."; Perito, *Where is the Lone Ranger When We Need Him? America's Search for a Postconflict Stability Force*: 112.Perito, *Where is the Lone Ranger When We Need Him? America's Search for a Postconflict Stability Force*: 112.

[27] There is great debate over the capability of Military Police to facilitate HNPA missions; however, the author believes that MPs fill a critical gap inherent to all HNPA missions. ————, *Where is the Lone Ranger When We Need Him? America's Search for a Postconflict Stability Force*: 1-2, 11; Jacqueline Chura-Beaver, "Developing Host Nation Law Enforcement Capacity for Security Transition," www.PKSOI.army.mil; "Host Nation Policing Advising Training Support Package: Police Advising Overview."; Nina Serafino, "Policing in Peacekeeping and Related Stability Operations: Problems and Proposed Solutions," Congressional Research Service, www.fas.org/man/crs/RL32321.pdf ; Seth Jones et al., "Establishing Law and Order After Conflict," RAND, http://www.rand.org/pubs/monographs/MG374.html.

[28] Ladwig, "Training Foreign Police: A Missing Aspect of U.S Security Assistance to Counterinsurgency," 288-91; "Host Nation Policing Advising Training Support Package: Police Advising Overview."

[29] Fitzgerald and Brady, "Considerations for the Employment of Transitional Law Enforcement Capabilities"; Chura-Beaver, "Developing Host Nation Law Enforcement Capacity for Security Transition"; "ICITAP Strategic Plan Fiscal Years 2009-2013".

The Clinton and Bush administrations each attempted to improve the USG's approach to HNPA as part of larger SSR reform efforts. Both presidents directed the department-level agencies to review the nation's partner capacity building missions and the manner in which government coordinated, funded, and facilitated these missions.[30] President Clinton issued Presidential Decision Directive 71 (PPD-71) in February 2000, in order to "'strengthen criminal justice systems in support of peace operations.'"[31] Although President Bush failed to re-issue PDD-71 he continued to support Peacekeeping Core Groups and strove to streamline interagency collaboration. The initiation of Operation Iraqi Freedom (OIF) made the lack of clear national guidance for HNPA apparent, leading President Bush to endorse Nation Security Presidential Directive 24, creating the Office of Reconstruction and Humanitarian Assistance. The National Security Council petitioned for the creation of this organization specifically to facilitate nation building.[32] These directives, and the National Defense Authorization Act of 1997, which called for the "establishment of an interagency cadre…" have all failed to draw the department-level agencies together in order to coordinate and collaborate.[33] The agencies repeatedly fail to collaborate or compromise, succumbing to internal rifts, and competing agendas, resulting in failed negotiations for the development of SSR and HNPA. Thus, due to poor USG coordination and integration, SSR remains a costly, complex, and challenging mission that rarely achieves its intended goals.[34] Meanwhile, in 2005 Secretary of Defense Donald Rumsfeld issued Department

---

[30] Perito, *Where is the Lone Ranger When We Need Him? America's Search for a Postconflict Stability Force.*

[31] Ibid., 239.

[32] Ibid., 278-79, 303.

[33] Quy Nguyen, "Swords and Plowshares: DOD and USAID on the Battlefield," *InterAgency Journal* 2, no. 2 (Summer 2011): 8-9.

[34] Agnes Hurwitz and Gordon Peake, "Strengthening the Security-Development Nexus: Assessing International Police and Practice Since the 1990s," International Peace Academy, www.ipacademy.org; James Locher, "The Most Important Thing: Legislature Reform of the National Security System," *Military Review* (May-June 2008): 19, 25-26; Nguyen, "Swords and Plowshares: DOD and USAID on the Battlefield," 10.

of Defense Directive 3000.05 directing the military to address stability operations, including security force assistance, as a "core mission." Unfortunately, this Directive, with DOD as the lone signatory, also failed to foster significant collaboration and coordination amongst the various department-level agencies, and simply increased the onus on the military to support and often execute SFA and SO with limited interagency involvement.[35] Until the department-level agencies come together, developing clear objectives, doctrine, and a common lexicon, with appropriate authorities and funding, the HNPA mission will continue to suffer from ad hoc execution.[36]

The USG must acknowledge the long-term demands of SSR and HNPA missions, if it intends SFA and building partner capacity to remain an American priority. The decision to authorize HNPA missions should include consideration of many factors to include the potential for the nation to adopt democratic ideals, the cost and time involved in recovering from the conflict, and the likelihood that long-term stability will flourish. Historically, SSR and HNPA take a minimum of five to ten years to effect long-term and enduring change.[37] Therefore, the success of these missions relies on the support of the department-level agencies, Congress, and the American people. SSR and HNPA also require long-term cooperation between the HN and the United States. Even with the necessary level of support and cooperation, it usually takes several years before one can gauge the likelihood of long-term success.[38]

To date, the USG has failed to improve SSR and HNPA policy and strategy, and the agencies have failed at the operational level to develop coherent and effective organizations to

---

[35] Department of Defense, "Department of Defense Instruction 3000.05," http://www.dtic.mil/whs/directives/corres/pdf/300005p.pdf; "U.S. Security".

[36] Perito, *Where is the Lone Ranger When We Need Him? America's Search for a Postconflict Stability Force*: 327.

[37] Jones et al., "Establishing Law and Order After Conflict"; Dilshika Jayamaha et al., *Lessons Learned From U.S. Government Law Enforcement In International Operations*, PKSOI Papers (Carlisle, PA: Strategic Studies Institute, 2010), 11.

[38] Chura-Beaver, "Developing Host Nation Law Enforcement Capacity for Security Transition".

implementation existing strategy and execute SSR and HNPA missions.[39] However, through a systematic approach including budgetary reform, clearly defined objectives, sound strategy, and effective programs, the USG could mitigate the shortfalls that currently detract from the conduct of HNPA at the operational level.[40]

HNPA missions depend greatly on the cultural context of the situation, which requires the personnel involved to understand the problem and the operational environment. Cultural context, historic perceptions, pre-intervention police effectiveness, and public confidence in local police all affect a nation's ability to accept and maintain a professional police force, capable of supporting the ROL. Therefore, the USG must tailor each HNPA mission to the specifics of its context to ensure success.[41] Additionally, successful large-scale HNPA operations require long-term support and commitment of both the HN and the American governments and societies, and require adequate resources provided throughout the duration of the mission. Both the USG and the HN must study the situation and understand it thoroughly to create the correct HNPA organization for the mission, and HN buy-in remains essential to the success of SSR or HNPA operations. Collectively, all elements involved must define the problem and support the proposals, in order for the strategies and programs to facilitate the effective and enduring establishment of ROL and community based policing.[42]

Although the USG has facilitated HNPA missions for decades, its efforts remain ad hoc and lack a solid base of institutional knowledge and lessons learned. Each mission requires an

---

[39] Strickler, "What the QDDR Says about Interagency Coordination," 67-70; Nguyen, "Swords and Plowshares: DOD and USAID on the Battlefield," 10.

[40] Henry Mintzberg, *The Rise and Fall of Strategic Planning* (New York: The Free Press, 1994), 89.

[41] Riegg, "Concepts and Systems for States in Crisis," 38; Martin, "Training Indigenous Security Forces at the Upper End of the Counterinsurgency Spectrum," 60.

[42] Hume and Miklaucic, "Exorcising Demons of the Past: Seizing New Opportunities to Promote Democratic Policing."; Jayamaha et al., *Lessons Learned From U.S. Government Law Enforcement In International Operations*: 112.

agency to seek out former participants or comb through archives as they develop their plan.[43] The lack of a formal means to assess past actions, in order to understand the components and phasing of the operation, resulted in failure of the USG to understand which types of operations proved successful, and why. Establishing a formal assessment system would enable the USG to identify the strengths and weaknesses of current and past programs and apply them to future missions, saving time and effort while improving overall effectiveness.[44]

In addition to the lack of institutional knowledge, the agencies also suffer from limited intelligence sharing. Intelligence shapes an agency's understanding of the environment, the culture, and context. Intelligence remains essential for the initial assessment of the situation, enabling sound decisions whether and how to institute SSR and HNPA missions. However, complications resulting from conflicting means of classification and operational security (OPSEC) concerns often prevent intelligence sharing. Effective intelligence sharing requires an integrated approach, and support from the parent agencies involved in HNPA missions. Additionally, the sharing of intelligence not only aids the implementation and execution of SSR and HNPA; it also enables critical assessment of the planning process. Finally, organizations must share intelligence amongst all elements involved, including the HN, to foster the mutual trust and transparency that enable long-term success.[45]

---

[43] Serafino, "Policing in Peacekeeping and Related Stability Operations: Problems and Proposed Solutions"; "ICITAP Strategic Plan Fiscal Years 2009-2013".

[44] "White Paper: Determining the Roles for General Purpose Forces and Special Operations Forces in Security Force Assistance Missions and Refining a Process for Identifying the Best Force for Specific SFA Missions," ed. JCISFA (Ft Leavenworth, KS: JCISFA, June 2008), 8; Stodiek, "OSCE's Police-Related Activities: Lessons Learned During the Last Decade," 205; Hume and Miklaucic, "Exorcising Demons of the Past: Seizing New Opportunities to Promote Democratic Policing."

[45] Jayamaha et al., *Lessons Learned From U.S. Government Law Enforcement In International Operations*: 156; Lawrence Yates, "Operation Just Cause in Panama City, December 1989," in *Block by Block: The Challenge of Urban Operations*, ed. William Robertson and Lawrence Yates (Fort Leavenworth, KS: U.S. Army Command and General Staff College Press, 2002); John Cockell, "Civil-Military Responses to Security Challenges in Peace Operations: Ten Lessons from Kosovo," *Global Governance*, no. 8 (2002): 497.

Just as organizations involved in SSR and HNPA missions lack leadership and intelligence sharing at the national level, they also lack leadership and an appropriate force structure at the operational level. In particular, HNPA needs a strong command and control structure with the appropriate resources for mission execution.[46] *FM 3-07, Stability Operations* defines command and control as "the exercise of authority and direction by a properly designated commander over assigned and attached forces in the accomplishment of a mission."[47] However, to date the USG has structured and led each HNPA operation differently, which in turn complicates all facets of the mission. Enacting consistent leadership and force structure would aid in the development of consistent, well-defined objectives, effective allocation of resources, and overall integration among all organizations involved in the mission. By pairing command and control with the appropriate force structure, the United States could finally achieve unity of effort, defined in *FM 3-07, Stability Operations*, as "the coordination and cooperation toward common objectives, even if the participants are not necessarily part of the same command or organization—the product of unified action." Collectively, these two principles would improve collaboration, coordination, and interoperability, resulting in an effective and efficient HNPA plan.[48]

Many means exist to improve existing command and control limitations, including creation of a new government agency charged with security sector reform, assigning an existing agency to oversee the fulfillment of all HNPA missions, or forming an HNPA Joint Interagency Coordination Group (JIACG) or a Joint Interagency Task Force (JIATF). Effective command and control improves unity of effort, fostering increased coordination and collaboration. JIATF South

---

[46] Perito, *Where is the Lone Ranger When We Need Him? America's Search for a Postconflict Stability Force*: 328; Cockell, "Civil-Military Responses to Security Challenges in Peace Operations: Ten Lessons from Kosovo," 487, 90.

[47] U.S. Army, "Field Manual 3-07, Stability Operations," Glossary 10, 3.

[48] Caldwell and Leonard, "Field Manual 3-07, Stability Operations: Upshifting the Engine of Change," 56, 59; Serafino, "Policing in Peacekeeping and Related Stability Operations: Problems and Proposed Solutions"; "U.S. Security".

and JIATF West, two command and control organizations already in place, have successfully led the counter narcotics interdiction mission throughout the Caribbean and Pacific oceans respectively.[49]

For a mission to succeed, it must have clearly defined objectives and a feedback mechanism that assesses progress and adjusts the plan accordingly to changes in the environment. Organizations conducting HNPA must establish assessment methods at the onset of the mission and enjoy the full support of both the HN and the USG.[50] These assessments, enabled by identification and evaluation of measures of performance and measures of effectiveness, provide HNPA mission participants with the insight necessary to adjust strategy and programming during HNPA execution. Planners must continually review and update these measurements throughout the execution of the HNPA mission to enable timely and effective changes to mission goals and execution.[51] Assessments, supported by institutional knowledge and intelligence, consistently prove essential to the long-term effectiveness and continual progress of an HNPA mission, and require a concerted effort by all participants to ensure the mission is not only tailored to the environment, but also that the plan evolves to address the needs of the situation.[52]

---

[49]Steven Canby, "Roles, Missions, and JTFs: Unintended Consequences," *Joint Forces Quarterly* (Autumn/Winter 1994-95).According to Steven Canby, JTFs decrease parochialism and increase synergy, coordination, and collaboration. These organizations also foster the development of common lexcon and standards across multiple serveices and agencies. Richard Yeatman, "JIATF-South: Blueprint for Success," *Joint Forces Quarterly*, no. 42 (3rd Quarter 2006).not only supports Canby's claims but emphasizes the fact that JTFs enable multiple agencies to work together, sharing information, and working around the challenges surrounding legal authorities and fundin. By seamlessly handing off certain data or tasks to specific JTF members, the group benefits and actions are both legal and consistent.

[50] Chura-Beaver, "Developing Host Nation Law Enforcement Capacity for Security Transition"; Stodiek, "OSCE's Police-Related Activities: Lessons Learned During the Last Decade," 208.

[51] U.S. Army, "FM 5-0 C1: The Operations Process, Change 1," (Washington, DC: Headquarters, Department of the Army, March 18, 2011), 1-3 - 1-5; "White Paper: Determining the Roles for General Purpose Forces and Special Operations Forces in Security Force Assistance Missions and Refining a Process for Identifying the Best Force for Specific SFA Missions," 6, 8.

[52] Hume and Miklaucic, "Exorcising Demons of the Past: Seizing New Opportunities to Promote Democratic Policing."; Martin, "Training Indigenous Security Forces at the Upper End of the Counterinsurgency Spectrum," 59-60.

The element that enables all of these reforms to work is the development and codification of HNPA doctrine. Doctrine serves as a guide for the planning and execution of an operation, by providing all participants with a common lexicon of clearly defined terms and methods, improving communication, unity of effort, and efficiency.[53] Consequently, the continued ad hoc execution of HNPA will waste the limited time and resources of the USG. Creation of HNPA doctrine would provide a base line for the planning, execution, and assessment of HNPA missions, and provide a means of reform by addressing the weaknesses in the USG's current approach to HNPA.[54]

Thus, as the importance of HNPA and SSR continues to grow and America's commitment in Iraq and Afghanistan subsides, the situation calls for a careful assessment of HNPA missions at the strategic and operational levels.[55] If the USG can stabilize and improve the security apparatus of failing states, it can help foster growth and development, resulting in greater, self-sustainable internal stability for the HN.[56] Additionally, a more effective and efficient means of HNPA and SSR planning and execution would allow for the transition from conflict to stability operations more rapidly, and potentially result in lower overall costs to accomplish SSR and HNPA missions.

The Significance of HNPA

Police serve as the cornerstone of a legitimate government's security apparatus, and the security they provide enables all other facets of governance to flourish, lending legitimacy to the

---

[53] U.S. Army, "FM 1-02: Operational Terms and Graphics," (Washington, DC: Headquarters, Department of the Army, September 2004), 1-65.

[54] Riegg, "Concepts and Systems for States in Crisis," 38; Serafino, "Policing in Peacekeeping and Related Stability Operations: Problems and Proposed Solutions".

[55] HNPA efforts continue to expand throughout Africa, the Middle East and Southern Asia.

[56] Caslen, "Change 1 to Field Manual 3-0 The Way the Army Fights Today," 87; Caldwell and Leonard, "Field Manual 3-07, Stability Operations: Upshifting the Engine of Change," 58; Department of Defense, "Sustaining U.S. Global Leadership: Priorities for 21st Century Defense," http://www.defense.gov/news/Defense_Strategic_Guidance.pdf.

state.[57] Through SSR, specifically HNPA, the DOD, DOS, and DOJ collectively provide assets and resources to failed or failing states. These efforts result in intervention in post conflict situations to re-establish security and state sovereignty or prevent the collapse of security, which would result in the inability of a government to protect and provide for its citizens. If properly implemented, USG efforts in SSR and HNPA can improve the security for not only the host nation, but also the global community. However, these remain complex missions. The USG must fully define when and how it will conduct SSR and HNPA before it can enact additional reforms.[58]

Critical Terms

Although SSR and HNPA continue to grow in importance to the nation's overall security efforts, the terms remain ill defined. Today, after decades of executing these missions in various locations and situations, the associated tasks and methods remain unclear, with each agency defining the key terms to suit its needs. However, the following study uses definitions contained in United States Army doctrine, unless otherwise noted.

The USG, led by the DOS, conducts SSR, which *FM 3-07, Stability Operations* defines as "policies, plans, programs, and activities that a government undertakes to improve the way it provides safety, security, and justice."[59] Development of ROL forms a significant component of SSR. *FM 3-07* defines ROL as "a principle under which all persons, institutions, and entities, private and public, including the state itself, are accountable to laws that are publically promulgated, equally enforced, and independently adjudicated and that are consistent with

---

[57] "Foreign Assistance Meeting the Training Needs of Police in New Democracies"; Ladwig, "Training Foreign Police: A Missing Aspect of U.S Security Assistance to Counterinsurgency," 285, 92; Bayley and Perito, *The Police in War: Sighting Insurgency, Terrorism, and Violent Crime*: 56.

[58] "ICITAP Strategic Plan Fiscal Years 2009-2013"; "Multiple U.S. Agencies Provided Billions of Dollars to Train and Equip Foreign Police Forces".

[59] U.S. Army, "Field Manual 3-07, Stability Operations," Glossary 9.

international human rights principles."[60] ROL, like SSR, requires an integrated collective effort by the USG department-level agencies – particularly the DOS, DOJ, and DOD. It enables sustainable peace and fosters development across the full spectrum of national power.[61] Establishing ROL requires prioritizing the synchronized and integrated development of police, justice, and prison systems that are legitimate in both the eyes of the people and the international community.[62]

The DOD, as a supporting element to DOS, conducts SO and SFA while supporting SSR. *FM 3-07, Stability Operations* defines stability operations as "an overarching term encompassing various military missions, tasks, and activities conducted outside the United States in coordination with the other instruments of national power to maintain or reestablish a safe and secure environment, provide essential government services, emergency infrastructure, and humanitarian relief." *FM 3-07* defines SFA as a component of SSR, as "the unified action to generate, employ, and sustain local, host-nation, or regional security forces in support of legitimate authority."[63]

Under SSR, the agencies work to build partner capacity, specifically targeting host-nation security forces. Although military forces generally perform the preponderance of mission tasks, police serve as the cornerstone to the establishment of long lasting stability. Where as the military serves as a "protector of the state…the police became primarily a crime-fighting actor, the enforcer of laws enacted to maintain social order," serving the people.[64] Police provide security for the people and the state, enabling development, stability, and growth. However, developing a

---

[60] Ibid.

[61] Elements of National Power include Diplomacy, Information, Military, and Economic.

[62] Perito, *Where is the Lone Ranger When We Need Him? America's Search for a Postconflict Stability Force.*

[63] U.S. Army, "Field Manual 3-07, Stability Operations," Glossary 9.

[64] Gerspacher, "The History of International Police Cooperation: A 150-year Evolution in Trends and Approaches," 178.

legitimate police force within a failed or failing state remains a challenge for the USG. To develop this pillar of the state's security triad, the agencies collectively conduct HNPA, a subset of SSR and SFA, and integral to ROL. By targeting the host-nation police force, the agencies can establish local security and stability, enabling the entirety of the SSR mission to blossom. HNPA includes the training, coaching, and mentoring of both police and corrections officers. Forces conducting HNPA must represent an integrated component of a more comprehensive effort focused on the reform of the nation's overarching judicial system, in order to deter, detect, and defeat crime.[65]

Forces conducting HNPA seek to institute democratic and community-based policing, for which the DOS has established the following criteria:

> (1) The actions of the police must be governed by law; (2) Police actions must not violate international principles of human rights; (3) The police must be subject to external supervision with respect to both corporate law enforcement effectiveness and the behavior of individual officers in the performance of their duty; (4) The police must be responsive to the needs of individual citizens.[66]

Democratic policing results in both accountable and transparent police agencies, which lends to the legitimacy of the state. Therefore, effective execution of HNPA missions requires a comprehensive and systematic approach to the establishment of ROL, prioritizing the synchronized and integrated development of police, justice, and prison systems that are legitimate in both the eyes of the people and the international community. HNPA cannot succeed without the successful execution of SSR, SO, and SFA, collectively striving to foster a stable, democratic state, operating under the ROL, capable of participating in the global community.[67]

---

[65] "Host Nation Policing Advising Training Support Package: Police Advising Overview."

[66] Hume and Miklaucic, "Exorcising Demons of the Past: Seizing New Opportunities to Promote Democratic Policing."

[67] Bayley and Perito, *The Police in War: Sighting Insurgency, Terrorism, and Violent Crime*: 130.

18

Purpose

The following analysis addresses both the strengths and weaknesses of historic HNPA missions in which DOS, DOJ, and DOD all participated, and the issues that continue to plague such missions. By identifying these elements, the USG can develop and institute a more effective system to facilitate future HNPA missions. The study focuses on alternate command and control structures, and programmatic and operational reforms the USG – particularly department-level agencies – must undertake to improve HNPA mission planning and effectiveness.[68] The study also reveals reforms the United States Army Military Police Corps can institute to improve their support to HNPA missions, particularly in the interim period between commencement of operations and arrival of other government agency resources and personnel.[69] Through the implementation of comprehensive reform, DOD, with the assistance of other USG agencies, can conduct HNPA missions more efficiently as both a pre-emptive and a post-conflict tool, capable of improving global stability and security.[70]

DOS serves as the lead agency for SSR; however, DOD and DOJ provide key support.[71] Although current policies and doctrine emphasize the growing importance of HNPA, the department-level agencies have failed to develop a comprehensive means to implement, plan,

---

[68] Bayley introduced the terms programmatic and operational in this book. He goes into detail about each and defines the components. The author has embraced these terms but has modified the components of each as described within the monograph.David Bayley, *Changing the Guard: Developing Democratic Police Abroad* (New York, NY: Oxford University Press, 2006), 133-34, 38-39.

[69] Fitzgerald and Brady, "Considerations for the Employment of Transitional Law Enforcement Capabilities"; Serafino, "Policing in Peacekeeping and Related Stability Operations: Problems and Proposed Solutions"; Locher, "The Most Important Thing: Legislature Reform of the National Security System," 19, 25.

[70] Riegg, "Concepts and Systems for States in Crisis," 40; Nguyen, "Swords and Plowshares: DOD and USAID on the Battlefield," 10; Locher, "The Most Important Thing: Legislature Reform of the National Security System."

[71] Caldwell and Leonard, "Field Manual 3-07, Stability Operations: Upshifting the Engine of Change," 59.

direct, or assess such missions.[72] To develop an effective HNPA program, these agencies must 1) improve their cooperation through integrated planning, before and during the conduct of HNPA missions, 2) implement programmatic changes addressing, in particular, authorities, lines of funding, and manning, and 3) revise the operational systems utilized, including planning, training, implementation, and assessment methods to achieve greater long term success.[73] Thus, the following analysis demonstrates that creation of a stable command and control element (i.e. lead agency, JIATF, or JIACG), capable of integrated planning, with the appropriate legal and funding authorities, supported by programmatic and operational change, will enable more effective HNPA by the United States government.

Methodology

One must understand HNPA missions in a larger SSR context. Fortunately, many sources exist, including journal articles, government reports, and independent assessments (primary and secondary sources from government agencies, Research and Development (RAND), and the Peacekeeping and Stability Operations Institute (PKSOI)) that provide insight into the conduct of SSR at the macro level and HNPA at the micro level. The references provide information and historic insight pertaining to the organizational planning, implementation, and assessment processes of the HNPA mission. In addition to historical context, research reveals the broad issues and challenges that lessen the overall effectiveness of HNPA operations. Finally, analysis of three case studies – the HNPA operations in Panama, Kosovo, and Haiti –highlights lessons learned and potential reforms that can improve the overall execution of HNPA missions by the USG.

---

[72] "National Security Strategy"; "Quadrennial Diplomacy and Development Review"; "Quadrennial Defense Review"; "The Army Capstone Concept"; U.S. Army, "Field Manual 3-07, Stability Operations."; ———, "Field Manual 3-07.1, Security Force Assistance."; ———, "ATTP 3-39.10 (FM 19-10), Law and Order Operations."

[73] Mintzberg, *The Rise and Fall of Strategic Planning*: 79-81.Here Mintzberg describes the gap in planning methods and through the application of both performance control and action planning methods; planners can bridge the great divide. This issue will be further addressed in the Methodology section.

To illustrate the challenges America faces in conducting effective HNPA operations, the following case study analysis assesses the problem through the lens of the two processes Henry Mintzberg describes as contrasting aspects of organizational planning. In his book *The Rise and Fall of Strategic Planning*, Mintzberg describes performance control and action planning as two different but integral components of planning or strategy development processes. Performance control "relies on existing organizational structures," providing a quantitative measurement focused on budgets and programs. Action planning, on the other hand, serves as a qualitative measure focused on the strategies and programs required to achieve certain goals. To plan and strategize effectively, organizations must integrate both methods.[74]

However, department-level agencies tend to rely on performance control for planning and strategy development. Performance control methods motivate and control subordinate organizations; however, this top-down approach hinders comprehensive strategy development. Performance controls provide broad objectives but suffer from limited flexibility and poor assessment mechanisms. Unlike the other departments, DOD frequently conducts action planning.[75] This method of planning facilitates a comprehensive approach to strategy development, and the implementation, execution, and assessment of strategies. While reality shapes performance control, conceptual thought shapes action planning. Mintzberg calls the contrast between these two methods the "great divide," a common problem that poses a significant challenge to SSR and HNPA planners, who are responsible for linking budgets and

---

[74] Ibid., 79, 86.

[75] Strickler, "What the QDDR Says about Interagency Coordination," 73; Justin Kelly and Mike Brennan, "Alien: How Operational Art Devoured Strategy," Strategic Studies Institute, http://www.strategicstudiesinstitute.army.mil/pubs/display.cfm?pubID=939.

objectives with tangible strategies and programs.[76] In order to bridge this divide, planners must integrate both performance controls and action planning methods.[77]

Evaluating the case studies to measure the quality of coordination and collaboration amongst the department-level agencies, and the method of planning and strategy development used, reveals challenges posed by the "great divide." This highlights means to improve development of SSR and HNPA strategy by bridging the divide, improving the strategic plans so they reflect an integrated approach to performance control and action planning.[78]

Performance control methods tend to place constraints on the development and implementation of the overall performance of a strategy. Budgetary matters and objectives shape the plan fostered through performance control methods. For example, budgetary limitations and inconsistent support habitually plague the execution of HNPA missions.[79] A myriad of USG agencies compete for limited funds provided on an annual basis and normally at varying levels each year. Therefore, agencies seeking to contribute to HNPA activities often find their plans constrained by inconsistent and unreliable funding.[80] In addition, agencies participating in HNPA missions lack clear authorities to guide the utilization of funds. Appropriate funding and authorities would enable the government to define and assess clear HNPA objectives, with appropriately monitored programs that support an integrated USG strategy.[81]

---

[76] Mintzberg, *The Rise and Fall of Strategic Planning*: 78-80.

[77] Ibid., 79-81; Wayne Grigsby et al., "Integrated Planning The Operations Process, Design, and the Military Decision Making Process," *Military Review* (January-February 2011): 28, 34.

[78] Although this monograph employs Mintzberg's concept of integrated planning, more recent publications emphasize integrated planning as well, reinforcing the validity of this approach. For example"Quadrennial Diplomacy and Development Review"; Kelly and Brennan, "Alien: How Operational Art Devoured Strategy"; Jan Schwarzenberg, "Where are the JIACGs Today," *InterAgency Journal* 2, no. 2 (Summer 2011); Matthew Johnson, William Smith, and William Farmen, "Mechanics of Governance Approach to Capacity Development," *InterAgency Journal* 2, no. 2 (Summer 2011).

[79] "Foreign Assistance Meeting the Training Needs of Police in New Democracies"; "U.S. Security".

[80] "ICITAP Strategic Plan Fiscal Years 2009-2013".

[81] Mintzberg, *The Rise and Fall of Strategic Planning*: 71-72.

Performance controls also address the objectives or endstate of an operation. Objectives guide the efforts of all organizations, explaining how the organizations will achieve the endstate. Currently, each agency providing some form of support to the HNPA mission defines its own objectives while also working toward common, broadly defined overall objectives.[82] This often results in redundant or even contradictory efforts. The lead agency must clearly define the objectives, dictating lines of effort and roles for each organization involved in order to build a unified approach toward HNPA missions. The overarching HNPA objectives must nest with the overall national security strategy, DOS's mission strategic resource plan for the region, and DOD's theater security plan for the specific Unified Combatant Command. Thus, the overall implementation and effectiveness of the HNPA mission rely on the awareness of the effect of performance controls, because they determine the resources available and the mission objectives, both of which serve as essential components of the framework of the overall plan.[83]

Although constraints frame performance control methods, an unconstrained approach inspires action planning. In other words, action planning provides the conceptual components for the implementation of the plan, unconstrained by the considerations of performance controls. Additionally, action planning provides a means to develop and assess strategies and programs. Strategies consist of unique concepts, often abstract in nature, intended to solve a problem or enable development of a plan for future operations. Programs, in turn, place strategies into action by providing details like a timeline of actions, milestones, and assessments. Together, strategies and programs provide decisive actions and actionable, assessable plans for execution.[84]

Strategy, in its abstract form, leads to a unique conception tailored to support a specific outcome or facilitate a specific plan. Strategy requires initiative and coordination amongst both

---

[82] "U.S. Security"; "Multiple U.S. Agencies Provided Billions of Dollars to Train and Equip Foreign Police Forces".

[83] ———, *The Rise and Fall of Strategic Planning*: 72-73.

[84] Ibid., 75.

leaders and subordinates. The department-level agencies lack strategy for the execution of SSR and HNPA missions.[85] Most government agencies develop broad strategy based on a funding cycle. However, to support effective HNPA efforts they must develop specific strategies to fit the needs of the HN tailored to each individual situation. Additionally, strategy development – a long-term endeavor – must remain relevant through recurring evaluation and adjustment, or it risks losing its effectiveness.[86] Therefore, while the USG may establish broad objectives and allocate funds for the execution of HNPA missions, the lack of action planners and conceptual strategy to direct the mission continues to hinder performance and effectiveness.[87]

Action planning not only facilitates the development of strategy; it also contributes to the development of programs. Programs enable the implementation and assessment of strategy. They often consist of timelines and milestones, and usually include a feedback mechanism to support assessments of both the programs themselves and the overall strategy.[88] The ad hoc nature of HNPA missions and the lack of institutional knowledge among many agencies supporting them result in programs developed without the benefit of integrating lessons learned.[89] Further, each individual agency conducting HNPA develops its own program, with little cross-agency coordination to prevent redundancy and disconnectedness.[90] Additionally, like strategy, programs depend on funding through annual budget allocations. This annual funding cycle often hinders

[85] Bayley, *Changing the Guard: Developing Democratic Police Abroad*: 128; Strickler, "What the QDDR Says about Interagency Coordination," 67, 70.

[86] "White Paper: Determining the Roles for General Purpose Forces and Special Operations Forces in Security Force Assistance Missions and Refining a Process for Identifying the Best Force for Specific SFA Missions," 6; "ICITAP Strategic Plan Fiscal Years 2009-2013".

[87] Mintzberg, *The Rise and Fall of Strategic Planning*: 75, 81.

[88] "White Paper: Determining the Roles for General Purpose Forces and Special Operations Forces in Security Force Assistance Missions and Refining a Process for Identifying the Best Force for Specific SFA Missions," 4, 8.

[89] Stodiek, "OSCE's Police-Related Activities: Lessons Learned During the Last Decade," 204; "ICITAP Strategic Plan Fiscal Years 2009-2013"; Bayley, *Changing the Guard: Developing Democratic Police Abroad*: 130.

[90] "Foreign Assistance Meeting the Training Needs of Police in New Democracies".

program development and long-term effectiveness. Thus, HNPA strategy and programs, as subsets of action planning, require integration with performance control elements in order to achieve greater success.[91]

In order to develop a comprehensive strategic plan for HNPA, the USG must integrate both performance control and action planning methods. This integrated approach will enable the establishment of a comprehensive and effective plan by bridging the "great divide" between conceptual and detailed planning. Most department-level agencies rely almost exclusively on performance control methods, which alone cannot lead to effective strategy formation. However, the DOD is capable of bridging the "great divide" in HNPA, through action planning and greater cooperation with elements of DOS and DOJ. Thus, analysis of the respective case studies reveals the effect of Mintzberg's performance control and action planning methods and their respective hierarchies (budget, objectives, strategy, and programs). This enables identification of a more integrated approach that will improve America's success in HNPA missions.

Case Studies

All three case studies involve HNPA missions conducted by ICITAP in partnership with DOD: Operation Promote Liberty in Panama, 1989-1990; Operation Uphold Democracy in Haiti, 1995-2000; and Kosovo Forces (KFOR) and the United Nations Interim Administration Mission in Kosovo (UNMIK), 1999-Present. The case studies facilitate analysis of the performance control and action planning measures that led to the manner of execution of each HNPA mission. Comparing and contrasting Mintzberg's four hierarchies described above enable identification of the strengths and weaknesses of each mission.[92] Finally, synthesis of the case studies supports

---

[91] Mintzberg, *The Rise and Fall of Strategic Planning*: 75.

[92] Mintzberg's four hierarchies are budget, objectives, strategy, and programs. Details are in the Methodology section.

several recommendations to improve both the planning process and the execution of HNPA missions by DOS, DOJ, and DOD.

Panama

The United States has a long history of involvement in Panama, centered on the defense of the Panama Canal throughout the twentieth century. U.S. forces maintained a robust military presence within the Central American nation through the late 1990s. This presence enabled American forces to train throughout the nation, often in partnership with the Panamanian Defense Forces (PDF), until the rise in Manuel Noriega's power and influence in the1980s strained relations between the two countries. Noriega took control of the PDF, ultimately achieving power as military dictator. In this role, Noriega used the PDF to safeguard his reign and to repress the people. This abuse of power caused Panamanians and many among the global community to view the PDF as synonymous with corruption and abuse of human rights. As conditions across Panama deteriorated and the erosion of democracy continued, tensions rose between the United States and the Government of Panama.[93]

In order to influence the situation, the United States Congress instituted in May 1989, economic and military measures against Panama, and worked to have Noriega deposed in order to reinstate a legitimate, democratic government.[94] This led Noriega to tighten control over Panama and increased tensions between the two nations, although diplomatic engagement continued through December 1989. These diplomatic engagements ultimately proved unsuccessful, but they provided time for the American military to develop options to force Noriega from power, with the

---

[93] Jennifer Morrison Taw, "Operation Just Cause: Lessons for Operations Other Than War," Arroyo Center, http://www.rand.org/pubs/monograph_reports/MR569 html.

[94] Ronald Cole, "Operation Just Cause: The Planning and Execution of Joint Operations in Panama February 1988-January 1990," (Washington, DC: Joint History Office, 1995), 10-13.The U.S. Military began planning for military operations to remove Noriega in February 1988; however, the U.S. Congress responded to Noriega's interference to the elections in May 1989. The impediment of democracy caused Congress to increase diplomatic efforts and renew interest in military options.

goal of reestablishing a legitimate government, protecting American lives, seizing and arresting indicted drug traffickers, and defending the integrity of American rights under the canal benefits.[95]

The DOD conducted deliberate and detailed planning for Operation Just Cause throughout 1989. The military conducted exercises, staged equipment and personnel in Panama, and continually refined the plan. Although DOD conducted thorough planning, it focused on combat operations. The military leaders failed to coordinate with the other department-level agencies and they failed to integrate the civil affairs plan for stability operations into the overall operational concept. Likewise, the department-level agencies failed to acknowledge the need for planning and preparation, despite the rising tensions in Panama and the abuse generated by Noriega's regime. Thus, the other agencies proved unprepared to support DOD's combat and stability operations, conducted between December 1989 and January 1990.[96]

On 20 December 1989, the United States invaded Panama, initiating Operation Just Cause, a joint, combined operation, designed to end forcefully Noriega's regime. This operation reflects the DOD's ability to bridge the great divide between Performance Control Methods and Action Planning Methods.[97] Regardless of the rapid success achieved during the invasion, the DOD failed to conduct similar planning for stability operations – the second phase of the mission, known as Operation Promote Liberty. United States military forces proved unprepared for this sudden shift in mission, the PDF could not secure and stabilize the nation, and the other USG

---

[95] Taw, "Operation Just Cause: Lessons for Operations Other Than War"; Yates, "Operation Just Cause in Panama City, December 1989," 47-49.

[96] Cole, "Operation Just Cause: The Planning and Execution of Joint Operations in Panama February 1988-January 1990," 65-67; Taw, "Operation Just Cause: Lessons for Operations Other Than War".

[97] Mintzberg, *The Rise and Fall of Strategic Planning*: 78.

department-level agencies had not prepared to support SSR and HNPA.[98] The USG failed to conduct either performance controls or action planning in order to successfully transition from combat operations to stability operations.[99]

Mintzberg defines performance controls as objectives and budgetary constraints. Operation Promote Liberty suffered from both ill-defined objectives and budgetary constraints. Objectives provide motivation and control, while depicting the desired endstate for all organizations involved. Although the USG clearly identified objectives for phase I, Operation Just Cause, with the establishment of security and governance "clearly stated in the mission statement of Operation Plan (OPLAN) 90-02," the DOD overlooked the importance and complexity of these tasks, and failed to define either objectives or resources for phase II, Operation Promote Liberty. [100]

DOD's incomplete planning effort resulted from the flawed assumption that the Panamanian government, through the PDF, would take the lead immediately upon transition to stability operations and create a safe and secure environment. However, the PDF disintegrated during conflict, leaving it unable and unwilling to provide security and support.[101] Ultimately, United States military leaders in Panama recognized they needed to transition to stability operations and identify clear objectives for Operation Promote Liberty, although initially the USG did not plan to conduct nation building operations.[102] Regardless, DOD recognized the

---

[98] Robert Mackey, "The Triple Threat In Operation Just Cause," *Military Police* (Winter 1990): 10; David Patton, "Operation Just Cause," (Fort Bragg, NC: Provost Marshal Office, 82nd Airborne Division, 1990), 4-6, 14.

[99] Taw, "Operation Just Cause: Lessons for Operations Other Than War"; Cole, "Operation Just Cause: The Planning and Execution of Joint Operations in Panama February 1988-January 1990," 65-67.

[100] Lawrence Yates, "Panama, 1988-1999: The Disconnect between Combat and Stability Operations," *Military Review* (May-June 2005): 49.

[101] ———, "Operation Just Cause in Panama City, December 1989."; Jayamaha et al., *Lessons Learned From U.S. Government Law Enforcement In International Operations*: 11,13-14.

[102] Perito, *Where is the Lone Ranger When We Need Him? America's Search for a Postconflict Stability Force*: 53; Jayamaha et al., *Lessons Learned From U.S. Government Law Enforcement In International Operations*: 11.

United States must reestablish both governance and security in order to safeguard American interests in the region.[103]

Objectives guide the overall accomplishment of the strategic mission; however, due to poor planning, lack of preparation, and delayed initiation of Operation Promote Liberty, Panama suffered from prolonged destabilization, looting, and violence.[104] After the rapid fall of Noriega and the PDF, the United States military quickly realized that it must reestablish a security apparatus.[105] Therefore, through crisis action planning, the DOD developed a means to achieve the initial stability objectives: establishment of security through the development and mentorship of the Panamanian National Police (PNP) and coordination with the United States Embassy (USEMB) country team, and the establishment of the Military Support Group (MSG) to facilitate the development of governance.[106]

Both the DOD and ICITAP failed to develop well-defined objectives, which would garner support from the HN and the organizations involved in the mission. Additionally, DOD and ICITAP initially failed to tailor the objectives to the context and culture of the populace involved. For example, although the PNP worked to maintain security, the populace saw them as a symbol of continued corruption and abuse, delaying the effectiveness of the PNP's operations and establishment of a legitimate government of Panama.[107] Therefore, by failing to define clear objectives or develop a plan appropriate to the situation, DOD and ICITAP alienated both the

---

[103] Perito, *Where is the Lone Ranger When We Need Him? America's Search for a Postconflict Stability Force*: 53.

[104] Taw, "Operation Just Cause: Lessons for Operations Other Than War".

[105] Laura Russell, "Restoring Law and Order," *Military Police* (Spring 1993): 8-9; Yates, "Panama, 1988-1999: The Disconnect between Combat and Stability Operations," 51-52; Cole, "Operation Just Cause: The Planning and Execution of Joint Operations in Panama February 1988-January 1990," 68.

[106] Taw, "Operation Just Cause: Lessons for Operations Other Than War"; Jayamaha et al., *Lessons Learned From U.S. Government Law Enforcement In International Operations*: 13-14,24.

[107] Roger Yochelson, "The International Criminal Investigative Training Assistance Program," Resource Library: The CBS Interactive Network, findarticles.com/p/articles/mi_m2194/is_n4_v62/ai_13859797; "ICITAP/Panama Police Training Project Evaluation: Final Report," (Arlington, VA: National Center for State Courts, August 1994), 3-4, 55.

government of Panama and the populace, ultimately delaying the implementation of an effective SSR and HNPA mission.

Due to its lack of a plan for the transition to stability operations, the USG failed to establish a budget and resources for Operation Promote Liberty. Budgets support both funding and resourcing of missions, to include personnel and equipment. Although DOD staged all of the resources for combat operations, it failed to prepare and stage resources for stability operations. Similarly, the other department-level agencies proved equally unprepared to support and facilitate stability operations and nation building. Thus, incomplete planning and preparedness for stability operations in Panama delayed budget development and resource allocation.[108]

The USG did not expect Operation Promote Liberty to last for ten years, but should have considered the protracted nature of HNPA and SSR missions, which require a concerted commitment by all organizations.[109] Although the USG spent well over $33 million on the PNP alone from 1989-1999, poor management resulted in inconsistent funding. This mismanagement resulted from ill-defined objectives and poor coordination amongst organizations.[110] Such budgetary constraints eventually forced the organizations to cooperate, clearly define the objectives, and prioritize projects, improving the long-term effectiveness of Operation Promote Liberty.[111]

Operation Promote Liberty's budgetary challenges included various resource constraints. Due to the rapid transition to stability operations and the poor integration of the department-level agencies, the military began collaborating with the PNP and worked to developed subordinate

---

[108] Garry Pittman and Dan Simpson, "Fighting Crime in Panama," *Military Police* (Spring 1993): 4.

[109] Jayamaha et al., *Lessons Learned From U.S. Government Law Enforcement In International Operations*: 11,19; Yates, "Panama, 1988-1999: The Disconnect between Combat and Stability Operations," 51.

[110] Taw, "Operation Just Cause: Lessons for Operations Other Than War"; "ICITAP/Panama Police Training Project Evaluation: Final Report," 3-4.

[111] "ICITAP/Panama Police Training Project Evaluation: Final Report," 3-4.

elements to facilitate nation building and security. However, the military lacked both the training necessary to equip soldiers to conduct stability operations, specifically HNPA, and the necessary authorization to train foreign national police. Consequently, within the first year, Congress emphasized and enforced FAA, Section 660, demanding the military transition its efforts to other department-level agencies. [112] Thus, DOS quickly identified ICITAP, a fledgling organization conducting limited police and judicial assistance throughout Central America, to take over the mission. [113] However, ICITAP proved grossly unprepared to execute the mission. They lacked personnel, interpreters, planning experience, and the many other resources necessary to re-establish ROL in Panama. ICITAP also lacked equipment with which to train the PNP or to issue the PNP so it could conduct independent operations. Fortunately, due to consistent funding and resourcing as well as the experience ICITAP gained throughout the course of the mission, the USG reestablished ROL in Panama, leading to the Government of Panama assuming the lead in the HNPA mission in 1994. [114]

Poor performance controls hindered the effectiveness of the SSR, HNPA mission in Panama, as reflected in the operation's ill-defined objectives and budgetary constraints – particularly upon transition to the stability phase. Through internal review and careful assessment, ICITAP and the USG worked to develop action planning in order to institute strategy and programs to accomplish the mission. [115] Action planning leads to clear strategies and programs, lacking in the initial plan. Once combined with the necessary budget, resources, and objectives to

---

[112] Jayamaha et al., *Lessons Learned From U.S. Government Law Enforcement In International Operations*: 23; Bayley and Perito, *The Police in War: Sighting Insurgency, Terrorism, and Violent Crime*: 34.

[113] ———, *The Police in War: Sighting Insurgency, Terrorism, and Violent Crime*: 34.

[114] "ICITAP/Panama Police Training Project Evaluation: Final Report," 10,12,60-61; Taw, "Operation Just Cause: Lessons for Operations Other Than War".

[115] Yochelson, "The International Criminal Investigative Training Assistance Program". "ICITAP/Panama Police Training Project Evaluation: Final Report," 42,45,60-61.

transition to stability operations, action planning meshed with performance controls, leading to an effective and efficient plan to accomplish the mission.

The delayed establishment of objectives in turn delayed the development of strategy. Strategy provides the overarching guidance for the accomplishment of HNPA, synchronizing the actions and efforts of all organizations. Although the military initially developed and instituted a strategy, it was not until ICITAP worked with the USEMB Team and the government of Panama that a more comprehensive strategy emerged.[116] The DOD's strategy focused on establishing stability operations, requesting and deploying selected military occupational specialties and reservists in order to support both governance and the establishment of security. The military also developed the MSG and Civilian Military Operations Centers (CMOC) to coordinate efforts, gain collaboration, and facilitate program execution. The MSG worked in conjunction with the government of Panama and the USEMB Team to develop a strategy and to link efforts and resources.[117] Thus, the strategy evolved with time, in step with the availability of greater resources.

As ICITAP arrived in 1990, the strategy blossomed, and the effectiveness of the PNP increased, "create[ing] a civil police force of high professional standing that will respect human rights and contribute to the institutionalization of democracy," through mentorship, monitors, and feedback.[118] Simultaneously, the department-level agencies focused on other facets of the security triad including justice and corrections. Although not equitably resourced or staffed, these efforts led to the establishment of security in Panama and the change in perception of both the PNP and

---

[116] "ICITAP/Panama Police Training Project Evaluation: Final Report," 60-61.

[117] Jayamaha et al., *Lessons Learned From U.S. Government Law Enforcement In International Operations*: 24-25; Yates, "Operation Just Cause in Panama City, December 1989."

[118] "ICITAP/Panama Police Training Project Evaluation: Final Report," 1.

the legitimacy of the Panamanian government.[119] This comprehensive strategy linked the objectives with the resources and the programs to develop the PNP fully. Although it took ten years, the strategy eventually led to an enhanced community based police force.[120]

Thus, success emerged in Panama incrementally and required a concerted long-term commitment and partnership at both the strategic and tactical levels. Once the USG identified the overarching objectives and strategies for Operation Promote Liberty, the leaders on the ground could develop programs to achieve the endstate. Initially, DOD implemented emergent measures, reacting to unanticipated events as they occurred. This led to their execution of programs limited in scope, focusing on the re-establishment of security and stability, the re-opening of police stations, and stability to enable other facets of SSR to flourish.[121] The military supported the vetting process of the PDF, conducted twenty hours of training with the former soldiers, and conducted joint patrols with the PNP.[122] Additionally, the military implemented a "guns for money program," opened hotlines for tips and intelligence, and worked to open lines of communication between the HN, the United States military and the other USG agencies.[123] These stunted efforts reflect poor planning, which in turn led to the commitment of limited personnel

---

[119] Yochelson, "The International Criminal Investigative Training Assistance Program"; Taw, "Operation Just Cause: Lessons for Operations Other Than War"; Stephen Green, "Augmentation Units in Panama," *Military Police* (Spring 1993): 11.

[120] "ICITAP/Panama Police Training Project Evaluation: Final Report," 1, 60-61; Perito, "U.S. Police in Peace and Stability Operations". Identifies success at two years post intervention; however, partnership lasted for ten years.

[121] _____, "U.S. Police in Peace and Stability Operations"; Kenneth Garrett, "In Both Jungle and Urban Operations," *Military Police* (Spring 1992): 41. Taw, "Operation Just Cause: Lessons for Operations Other Than War".

[122] Jayamaha et al., *Lessons Learned From U.S. Government Law Enforcement In International Operations*: 21-22; Anthony Schilling, "Law and Order South of the Border," *Military Police* (Winter 1990): 14.

[123] Patton, "Operation Just Cause," 34. Yates, "Panama, 1988-1999: The Disconnect between Combat and Stability Operations," 52; Cole, "Operation Just Cause: The Planning and Execution of Joint Operations in Panama February 1988-January 1990," 66-69.

and resources to the establishment of Operation Promote Liberty.[124] These efforts assisted the PNP at the tactical level; however, the military lacked the ability to mentor senior leaders within the PNP or assist in the establishment of the multitude of institutions required to support ROL and the full spectrum of policing operations.[125]

Once ICITAP took the lead, the USG looked for a more robust and comprehensive strategy. ICITAP initiated a four-month training academy for vetted PDF members, in order to focus on human rights and pro-active, community-based policing methods.[126] By 1991, over 5,500 PNP graduated from the academy. Unfortunately, both ICITAP and the PNP suffered from significant rates of turnover and poor executive level leadership. ICITAP implemented programs to resolve the issues, with the assistance of the Federal Bureau of Investigation (FBI), which first identified them through its assessment process.[127] By shoring up the institutions and administrative sections of both the PNP and the judicial and corrections system, the security triad grew into a stable, effective, reputable force. ICITAP lacked long-range planning and iterative reviews but eventually, as ICITAP improved its own internal programs and mechanisms, they were able to bolster the PNP. After ten years, the American military, the USEMB Team, and ICITAP finally integrated their actions and possessed the necessary resources to achieve their desired effects.[128]

The eventual success of SO and HNPA in Panama should not obscure the inconsistency and inefficiency of these efforts, particularly in the early stages. Had the department-level agencies heeded the guidance in OPLAN 90-02 and prepared for SO and HNPA in an integrated

---

[124] Green, "Augmentation Units in Panama," 11.

[125] Yates, "Panama, 1988-1999: The Disconnect between Combat and Stability Operations," 47-49; "ICITAP/Panama Police Training Project Evaluation: Final Report," 1-3, 60-61.

[126] Yochelson, "The International Criminal Investigative Training Assistance Program".

[127] "ICITAP/Panama Police Training Project Evaluation: Final Report," 42,45,60-61.

[128] Yates, "Panama, 1988-1999: The Disconnect between Combat and Stability Operations," 52; Perito, "U.S. Police in Peace and Stability Operations".

manner, the mission might have proceeded with fewer set backs.[129] The military, although unprepared for the rapid transition to stability operations, conducted crisis action planning to establish the initial strategy and programs for the HNPA. However, effective SSR and HNPA require other agencies' cooperation with DOD.[130] Eventually, ICITAP assumed the lead, but the mission still suffered from undefined objectives and budget constraints.[131] These performance control issues hindered strategy and program development. Ultimately, over the course of ten years, the PNP developed into an effective and respected security apparatus.[132] Nevertheless, had the USG conducted integrated planning for Operation Promote Liberty as effectively as it did for Operation Just Cause, it could have accomplished a much smoother transition from combat to stability operations, structured by clearly defined objectives and resources. This would have averted the security gap, encouraged rapid integration of United States department-level agencies, and set conditions for effective SSR and HNPA operations prior to the transition to stability operations.

Haiti

In December 1990, the Haitian people elected Jean-Bertrand Aristide as their first democratically elected president, with the hope that he would institute democratic values and reorganize the Haitian government and security apparatus.[133] However, before Aristide could institute any effective reforms Lieutenant General Raoul Cedras conducted a coup and assumed

---

[129] Cole, "Operation Just Cause: The Planning and Execution of Joint Operations in Panama February 1988-January 1990," 74; Taw, "Operation Just Cause: Lessons for Operations Other Than War".

[130] Jayamaha et al., *Lessons Learned From U.S. Government Law Enforcement In International Operations*: 13-15; Patton, "Operation Just Cause," 44.

[131] "ICITAP/Panama Police Training Project Evaluation: Final Report," 3.

[132] Yates, "Panama, 1988-1999: The Disconnect between Combat and Stability Operations," 52; "ICITAP/Panama Police Training Project Evaluation: Final Report," 1,4; Perito, "U.S. Police in Peace and Stability Operations".

[133] Sarah Meharg and Aleisha Arnusch, "Security Sector Reform: A Case Study Approach to Transition and Capacity Building," Strategic Studies Institute, http://www.strategicstudiesinstitute.army.mil/.

control of Haiti. This coup resulted in the repression of the Haitian people and abuse by a

dictator. Yet, in 1993, the United Nations (UN) and the Organization of American States (OAS)

brokered the Governor's Island Agreement between Aristide and Cedras.[134] This agreement

eventually led to in the transition of power from Cedras back to Aristide, under the purview of the

international community. The UN assumed the lead in this peacekeeping mission in order to

establish a safe and secure environment, return the legitimate government to power, and prepare

the nation for future democratic elections. However, when the international community attempted

to enforce the Governor's Island Agreement, Haitians refused to allow the UN forces to dock at

the island.[135] Therefore, in 1994 the USG prepared to invade Haiti, directing the DOD to develop

two plans: one for a forcible entry and another for a permissive entry into Haiti, with either

followed by a military occupation of the nation. Regardless which plan DOD implemented, it

sought the primary goal of restoring order and enabling the UN to enforce the Governor's Island

Agreement.

While the international community, especially the United States, applied all elements of

national power, they concurrently planned for the use of force, as a last resort. Operation Uphold

Democracy began in earnest in July 1994, when the DOD began planning military operations as

diplomatic efforts and economic sanctions continued. While the military led the integrated USG

planning efforts, the other department-level agencies, the UN, and even elements within the

Haitian government, developed plans to compliment and support the military actions. Thus, on

September 19, 1994 the United States led a multinational effort to enforce a UN Mandate and to

assist in the transition of power from Cedras back to Aristide, enforcing the principles of the

---

[134] Johanna Mendelson-Forman, "Security Sector Reform in Haiti," *International Peacekeeping* 13, no. 1 (March 2006): 16-17.

[135] Timothy JG Ho, "Ordering Disorder: An Evaluation of the Effectiveness of International Civilian Police Training in Haiti, 1994-2001" (Royal Roads University, 2006), 25-27. "Operation Uphold Democracy: US Forces in Haiti," (Norfolk, VA: U.S. Atlantic Command, May 1997), 1-2.

Governor's Island Agreement. Operation Uphold Democracy ultimately returned Aristide to power while also providing a safe and secure environment for the Haitian people.[136]

As the international community attempted to utilize diplomatic and economic means to institute the Governor's Island Agreement from July 1993 through September 1994, the USG prepared contingency plans for employing military power to enforce the agreement. This extended planning period allowed for both the military and the department-level agencies to assess the situation and prepare for the invasion of Haiti.[137] All organizations looked at performance control elements, identifying objectives and budgetary constraints, for the entire mission. The performance control elements within the UN mandate also provided clear motivation and control for all organizations involved.[138]

For the initial phase of the operation, the UN mandate and Governor's Island Agreement provided the objectives. The UN hoped to re-instate Aristide and to establish a safe and secure environment in order to facilitate democratic elections while strengthening the Haitian Government and monitoring, restructuring, and reforming the national security apparatus.[139] While planning for the mission, the USG revisited the lessons learned in Panama. Applying such historic lessons, the United States, and the international community prepared to implement HNPA within a greater SSR mission.[140] Accomplishing these broad objectives required a concerted, long-term, multiphase approach by the Multinational Force (MNF) and the USG.[141]

---

[136] David Stahl, "Operation Uphold Democracy Operations in Haiti August 1994 thru January 1995 " (Fort Eustic, VA: Training and Audiovisual Support Center), 10-14. "Operation Uphold Democracy: US Forces in Haiti," iv,2.

[137] _____, "Operation Uphold Democracy Operations in Haiti August 1994 thru January 1995 " 11; "Operation Uphold Democracy: US Forces in Haiti," iv, 5.

[138] Mintzberg, *The Rise and Fall of Strategic Planning*: 71.

[139] Meharg and Arnusch, "Security Sector Reform: A Case Study Approach to Transition and Capacity Building".

[140] Bayley and Perito, *The Police in War: Sighting Insurgency, Terrorism, and Violent Crime*: 39.

[141] "Operation Uphold Democracy: US Forces in Haiti," iv,5,14.

Unfortunately, these objectives failed to achieve the much-needed external support or motivate the government of Haiti to expand it efforts. The mission in Haiti consisted of multiple phases. In the first phase, the MNF led the effort to establish security and stability.[142] The second phase began with the assumption of command for the mission by the UN. The third and final phase transitioned the mission to the government of Haiti, with appropriate supervision and continued financial support.[143] The UN and the Government of Haiti never clearly defined objectives for the second and third phases, which led to redundancy and uncoordinated efforts. Additionally, these vague objectives proved difficult to measure and assess, which eventually led to poor action planning by the organizations involved.[144]

Not only were the objectives broad in scope and ill defined, the international community hoped to complete the mission in an unrealistic timeline.[145] The UN published revised mandates every six months. However, this method did not provide adequate long-range guidance given the enduring nature of the operation. Additionally, the USG wanted to avoid mission creep and hoped to set conditions for a rapid transition from the MNF to the UN.[146] Thus, the USG over-emphasized speed as the mission wore on. This desire to proceed rapidly led to inadequate assessments, poor integration of all partners including the Haitian government, and resulted in the

---

[142] The United States was a member of the Multinational Force (MNF)

[143] Meharg and Arnusch, "Security Sector Reform: A Case Study Approach to Transition and Capacity Building"; "Operation Uphold Democracy: US Forces in Haiti," 22,27-28.

[144] Janice Stromsem and Joseph Trincellito, "Building the Haitian National Police: A Retrospective and Prospective View," The Haiti Program, http://trincellito.com/user/HNPTrinity.final.pdf; Meharg and Arnusch, "Security Sector Reform: A Case Study Approach to Transition and Capacity Building". Stahl, "Operation Uphold Democracy Operations in Haiti August 1994 thru January 1995 " 13-16.

[145] "Operation Uphold Democracy: US Forces in Haiti," iv.

[146] Bayley and Perito, *The Police in War: Sighting Insurgency, Terrorism, and Violent Crime*: 37; Ho, "Ordering Disorder: An Evaluation of the Effectiveness of International Civilian Police Training in Haiti, 1994-2001," 29-30; Stahl, "Operation Uphold Democracy Operations in Haiti August 1994 thru January 1995 " 14,88,92.

acceptance of minimum standards before transitioning to the next phase.[147] Therefore, the

detailed and integrated initial phase, despite its clearly defined objectives, led to short lived

success.[148] The successively vague objectives failed to focus the efforts of all personnel involved

and failed to guide and motivate the organizations toward long-term success of the Haitian

security forces.[149]

The UN established a new budget every six months, to support each set of short-term

objectives. Such budgets consist of both monetary support and provisions for resource and

personnel management. Success in Haiti required the international community to make a long-

term commitment, yet with ill-defined objectives and limited signs of success the commitment of

both nations and organizations waned.[150] This demonstrates the criticality of the budget to the

success of a long term SSR or HNPA mission, which in this case required a steadfast

commitment from the HN, participating organizations, and the international community. In Haiti,

the budget rested on the success of the mission. During the initial phase, the mission appeared

successful, and therefore it received plentiful fiscal support.[151] However, as the mission waned so

too did the money and resources.[152]

Resource constraints, to include personnel and equipment hampered the mission in Haiti.

The MNF conducted the mission initially, providing security, stability, mentorship, and

---

[147] Meharg and Arnusch, "Security Sector Reform: A Case Study Approach to Transition and Capacity Building".

[148] Stahl, "Operation Uphold Democracy Operations in Haiti August 1994 thru January 1995 " 22. "Operation Uphold or Something: Haiti (U.S. Military Intervention)," http://www.highbeam.com/doc/1G1-15768453.html.

[149] "Operation Uphold or Something: Haiti (U.S. Military Intervention)"; Stromsem and Trincellito, "Building the Haitian National Police: A Retrospective and Prospective View".

"Haiti in Extremis," *The Christian Century* (March 1, 2000).[150] Mendelson-Forman, "Security Sector Reform in Haiti," 15.

[151] Meharg and Arnusch, "Security Sector Reform: A Case Study Approach to Transition and Capacity Building".

[152] Ho, "Ordering Disorder: An Evaluation of the Effectiveness of International Civilian Police Training in Haiti, 1994-2001," 33,39,63,66; Meharg and Arnusch, "Security Sector Reform: A Case Study Approach to Transition and Capacity Building".

assistance, but the transition to the UN and Civilian Police International (CIVPOL) led to a reduction in personnel and resources.[153] The efforts became poorly synchronized and inconsistent and the turn over in both the UN Staff and the HNP Staff significantly reduced the focus and quality of the HNPA mission. The limited number of trainers, mentors, and advisors, especially within the administrative and institutional components of the HNP, also severely limited the long-term success of the mission in Haiti.[154] Such resource constraints prohibited the HNP from developing and from successfully maintaining security and stability in Haiti.[155] Thus, both budgetary and resource challenges limited the overall success of the HNPA mission in Haiti.

The performance controls shape the mission through constraints, while action planning relies more on creativity, adaptability, and a progressive approach to mission planning. Action planning consists of strategy and program development, which facilitate a desired endstate.[156] Due to the extended planning horizon, the DOD conducted comprehensive action planning. The other department-level agencies also conducted planning; however, their planning proved less focused, poorly synchronized, and more theoretical than DOD's.[157] Action planning drives the development of strategy, while strategy itself is comprised of programs, generally arrayed along a timeline. Collectively, strategy and programs enable the achievement of objectives.

---

[153] Stromsem and Trincellito, "Building the Haitian National Police: A Retrospective and Prospective View".

[154] Ibid., 8. "Haiti in Extremis," 96; Meharg and Arnusch, "Security Sector Reform: A Case Study Approach to Transition and Capacity Building".

[155] Ho, "Ordering Disorder: An Evaluation of the Effectiveness of International Civilian Police Training in Haiti, 1994-2001," 63,66; Stromsem and Trincellito, "Building the Haitian National Police: A Retrospective and Prospective View".

[156] Mintzberg, *The Rise and Fall of Strategic Planning*: 78-79.

[157] "Operation Uphold Democracy: US Forces in Haiti," iv,5-9; Stahl, "Operation Uphold Democracy Operations in Haiti August 1994 thru January 1995 " 10,22,28.

The strategy in Haiti consisted of both SSR and HNPA efforts to improve various

ministries including the ministries of justice, defense, and interior.[158] Unfortunately, the UN and

the Government of Haiti developed strategies and programs within significant time and budgetary

constraints, without developing clear objectives and overarching endstates. Therefore, the

international community failed to develop a long-term, comprehensive, and well-resourced

strategy for Haiti, resulting in overall failure.[159]

Initially, the MNF based the strategy on the objectives established during the Governor's

Island Agreement and the lessons learned from the invasion of Panama in 1989. Regardless,

security and stability served as the initial priorities. To achieve these initial priorities the USG

persuaded Haiti to refrain from disbanding the Haitian military until a combined committee could

vet and select personnel to establish the Interim Public Security Force (IPSF).[160] The IPSF, under

the watchful eye of the International Police Monitors (IPM) would then establish and maintain

public order until the newly formed and trained Haitian National Police (HNP) could assume the

mission. To conduct this strategy, first the MNF facilitated security and stability while working to

set the conditions for agencies, including ICITAP, the UN, and CIVPOL, to expand the approach

and conduct SSR and HNPA in full.[161]

The MNF achieved success initially, as seen in the military and the IPSF patrolled

together establishing both security and stability.[162] Unfortunately, this success proved short-lived.

The MNF and ICITAP could not field the HNP rapidly enough or in great enough numbers to

---

[158] Steffan, "Multinational Force Haiti: Operation Uphold Democracy and 10th Mountain Division Operations in Haiti," ed. US Army War College (Center For Army Lessons LearnedFebruary 28, 1995). Meharg and Arnusch, "Security Sector Reform: A Case Study Approach to Transition and Capacity Building".

[159] Mendelson-Forman, "Security Sector Reform in Haiti," 15,22-25.

[160] Bayley and Perito, *The Police in War: Sighting Insurgency, Terrorism, and Violent Crime*: 38.

[161] Stahl, "Operation Uphold Democracy Operations in Haiti August 1994 thru January 1995 " 88, 92-97; "Operation Uphold Democracy: US Forces in Haiti," 27-28.

[162] Bayley and Perito, *The Police in War: Sighting Insurgency, Terrorism, and Violent Crime*: 39.

continue to secure the nation. Additionally, the Haitian populace did not trust or respect the HNP, despite the strides they made in community based policing.[163] This cultural perception indicated the inability of the international community to understand the cultural context of the situation and to tailor HNP development for the environment.[164] Strategy requires a collaborative effort between the HN and the international community, in order to capture the unique needs of the nation state. Unfortunately, the UN failed to assess properly the situation and adjust the strategy accordingly, and progress slowed.[165] The UN also failed to assess the cultural context of the situation. The UN's plan never gained support of the local populace or adequately addressed the issues plaguing the Government of Haiti. The HN population never accepted the HNP, resulting in mission paralysis. The mission in Haiti suffered from an inappropriate strategy as well as an under resourced and corrupt government unable to lead the nation effectively. Without a true partnership and a clear strategy, SSR and HNPA stalled and progress ceased.[166]

The UN recognized the need for a strategy that addressed the government of Haiti's security triad: police, justice, and prison reform; however, the UN failed to synchronize its efforts in these three key areas.[167] Thus, while the HNP began to develop, the justice and prison sectors lagged, further demoralizing the HNP and delegitimizing the government as a whole in the eyes

---

[163] Perito, *Where is the Lone Ranger When We Need Him? America's Search for a Postconflict Stability Force*: 111-12; Mendelson-Forman, "Security Sector Reform in Haiti," 24.

[164]_____, "Security Sector Reform in Haiti," 20; Meharg and Arnusch, "Security Sector Reform: A Case Study Approach to Transition and Capacity Building". Ho, "Ordering Disorder: An Evaluation of the Effectiveness of International Civilian Police Training in Haiti, 1994-2001," 10, 66.

[165] "Operation Uphold Democracy: US Forces in Haiti," 7; Stromsem and Trincellito, "Building the Haitian National Police: A Retrospective and Prospective View".

[166]Mendelson-Forman, "Security Sector Reform in Haiti," 89-90; "Haiti in Extremis," 228. ibid., 227-28; "Operation Uphold Democracy: US Forces in Haiti," 60-61.

[167] Stromsem and Trincellito, "Building the Haitian National Police: A Retrospective and Prospective View"; Meharg and Arnusch, "Security Sector Reform: A Case Study Approach to Transition and Capacity Building".

42

of the people.[168] By 2000, violence and corruption challenged democracy in Haiti and the SSR strategy, including the HNPA mission.[169]

Throughout the mission, strategy development and execution suffered from a lack of collaboration and integration amongst the agencies and the HN. Additionally, the broad scope of the mission resulted in a wide range of poorly synchronized, under-resourced, and ineffective efforts.[170] However, in 1996 the HNP, in collaboration with the international community, developed a five-year plan.[171] Unfortunately, HNPA efforts still failed to achieve long-term success because the Government of Haiti and the UN neglected to incorporate the justice and prison sectors into the plan. Only through a holistic approach based on integrated planning, careful assessments, detailed objectives, and proper resource management will Haiti's strategy achieve long-term success.[172]

The international community executed the SSR and HNPA strategy through a series of programs. Initially, the MNF implemented and facilitated a limited number of programs, to include joint patrols with the IPSF, training for the IPSF, and vetting and recruiting programs for the HNP all supported by Military Police and IPMs.[173] The IPMs had the authority to conduct law and order (L&O), and worked alongside the IPSF, guiding, mentoring, and monitoring the fledgling agency. IPMs also provided critical assessments on the conduct and capability of the HNP at the tactical level.[174] ICITAP, on the other hand, focused on strategic issues like the

---

[168] ———, "Security Sector Reform: A Case Study Approach to Transition and Capacity Building"; "Operation Uphold Democracy: US Forces in Haiti," 61.

[169] Stromsem and Trincellito, "Building the Haitian National Police: A Retrospective and Prospective View".

[170] Ibid., 1, 10.

[171] Ibid., 9.

[172] Ibid., 3,8; "Operation Uphold Democracy: US Forces in Haiti," 9, 60.

[173] Patrick Lafferty, "The 511th Mlitary Police Company in Cap Haitian, Haiti," *Military Police* (Winter 1995): 20.

[174] Perito, *Where is the Lone Ranger When We Need Him? America's Search for a Postconflict Stability Force*: 111-12; "Operation Uphold Democracy: US Forces in Haiti," 27-28.

HNP's institutional development, and established a four-month training academy.[175] Moreover, to assist in the establishment of ROL, prioritizing the synchronized and integrated development of police, justice, and prison systems that are legitimate in both the eyes of the people and the international community, the military established Military Assistance Teams (MATs), built around reservists with specialized skills and experience, in order to foster governance and ministerial development.[176] These early MNF efforts led to security and stability, which established the conditions for the transition to the UN.[177]

These early combined efforts achieved only short-term success. Unlike the USG, the UN did not conduct integrated planning, which led to a lack of preparation evident as soon as they assumed responsibility for the mission. For example, the UN instituted programs to support the HNP but they neglected the administrative and institutional needs of the organization.[178] By establishing a hollow force, the UN failed to create an organization capable of long-term sustainment and ultimate success.[179] Likewise, CIVPOL failed to sustain the multitude of programs established for SSR due to limited resources, waning international support, and the continued ineffectiveness of the Haitian government.[180] Thus, while the MNF achieved early success, the overall UN mission failed because of poor planning, an under resourced strategy, and unsynchronized programs.

---

[175] Stahl, "Operation Uphold Democracy Operations in Haiti August 1994 thru January 1995 " 92-97; "Operation Uphold Democracy: US Forces in Haiti," 27-28.

[176] Steffan, "Multinational Force Haiti: Operation Uphold Democracy and 10th Mountain Division Operations in Haiti."; "Operation Uphold Democracy: US Forces in Haiti," 41-42.

[177] _____, "Multinational Force Haiti: Operation Uphold Democracy and 10th Mountain Division Operations in Haiti."; Stahl, "Operation Uphold Democracy Operations in Haiti August 1994 thru January 1995 " 14,88,92.

[178] Ho, "Ordering Disorder: An Evaluation of the Effectiveness of International Civilian Police Training in Haiti, 1994-2001," 72-74. Stromsem and Trincellito, "Building the Haitian National Police: A Retrospective and Prospective View".

[179] The HNP lacked executive level leadership, training for senior officials, and insitutional support.Ho, "Ordering Disorder: An Evaluation of the Effectiveness of International Civilian Police Training in Haiti, 1994-2001," 63,72; Mendelson-Forman, "Security Sector Reform in Haiti," 22-25.

[180] "Haiti in Extremis," 227.

HNPA succeeds when the civilians the organization serves judge it successful.[181] In Haiti, the people did not see the HNP as a respected and effective organization. Nor did they consider the Haitian government a successful and legitimate organization. The international community must unite performance controls and action planning accounting for cultural and programmatic issues through integrated planning, to conduct successful SSR and HNPA missions. In Haiti, the mission ultimately dissolved due to poorly defined objectives, significant budgetary constraints, uncoordinated strategies and programs, and lack of support by the Government of Haiti. The inability of the international community to capitalize on the MNF's early success, lead to wavering support and commitment to the mission, therefore failing to achieve its objectives.[182]

KFOR/UNMIK

The United States and North Atlantic Treaty Organization (NATO) strove diplomatically, from 1998 thru 1999, to end the ethnic violence between the Albanian guerillas and the Yugoslav and Serb forces throughout the Kosovo Province. In 1999, NATO initiated Operation Allied Force, an air campaign against Slobodan Milosevic's Serbia and Yugoslav forces. Milosevic soon withdrew his forces from the Kosovo Province and the UN issued Security Council Resolution 1244, assuming "ultimate political authority" over the region. The United States, although not a participant in Operation Allied Force, elected to send peacekeeping forces under the UN Resolution. Collectively, the United States and NATO formed Kosovo Force (KFOR) to assist United Nation Interim Administrative Mission in Kosovo (UNMIK) with the implementation of Resolution 1244.[183]

---

[181] Ho, "Ordering Disorder: An Evaluation of the Effectiveness of International Civilian Police Training in Haiti, 1994-2001," 90.

[182] Meharg and Arnusch, "Security Sector Reform: A Case Study Approach to Transition and Capacity Building"; "Operation Uphold Democracy: US Forces in Haiti," 60-61.

[183] Steven J Woehrel and Julie Kim, "Kosovo and US Policy," Congressional Research Service, www.fas.org/sgp/crs/row/RL31053.pdf ; Jones et al., "Establishing Law and Order After Conflict".

The multinational force entered the Kosovo Province knowing that they must put an end to the ethnic violence; however, they also arrived prepared to conduct SSR. Through SSR, the international community worked to establish a functioning, independent, legitimate government and a level of security conducive to the resumption of normal daily activities within the Kosovo Province. ICITAP, a USG agency under DOJ, began planning for SSR prior to the declaration of Resolution 1244, developing a comprehensive plan for the establishment and development of a security force. However, the UN decided to assign the HNPA mission to UNMIK, not ICITAP. This decision ultimately delayed the implementation of HNPA.[184]

Despite initiating operations based on a well-prepared plan, the multinational force struggled with the implementation of both security and governance throughout the Kosovo Province. Initially, the UN made great strides in the establishment of the Kosovo Police Services (KPS); however, the endstate for the overarching UN mission remained undefined and Kosovo struggled to sustain the police force and to keep ethnic violence at bay. The challenges hindering the success of the HNPA mission in Kosovo stemmed from the constraints found within the performance control measures, and the UN and KFOR's delayed integration of performance control and action planning methods into the Resolution and successive mandates.

In Kosovo, the planners developing performance control methods failed to provide adequate guidance and support to the mission. The UN failed to define clear long-term objectives. For example, Resolution 1244 did not provide a specific endstate for the UNMIK mission in Kosovo. It simply stated, "Kosovo's final status to be considered at an undetermined time after an autonomous government is in place."[185] Therefore, the mandate sending forces into the region failed to provide a clear endstate from which to derive objectives. Thus, until UNMIK and KFOR

_____

[184] Jayamaha et al., *Lessons Learned From U.S. Government Law Enforcement In International Operations*: 108.

[185] Woehrel and Kim, "Kosovo and US Policy". Fortunately, the DOD conducted crisis action planning and the MPs provided immediate security and support to HNPA.

implemented the Kosovo Standards Implementation Plan, they could not develop adequate strategies and the mission continuously suffered from time delays, poor coordination, and poor assessments.[186]

The United States, unlike the UN, established clear long-term policy guidance and objectives from the beginning. The DOS developed objectives that reflected not only a decade of experience in HNPA missions but also took into consideration the capabilities resident in DOS, DOJ, and DOD.[187] Unfortunately, the USG proved as unprepared as the UN to support and execute the HNPA mission in Kosovo. The USG did not have police mentors at hand for immediate integration into post-conflict operations and did not conduct integrated planning to refine the mission and determine the overall requirements.[188] Additionally, while the DOD knew what objectives DOS identified for the mission, it remained focused on peacekeeping operations rather than the SFA and HNPA mission. This limited the effectiveness of department-level coordination, delaying the establishment of DOS objectives and resource allocation. However, once the departments defined these critical planning factors, coordination and collaboration amongst the agencies enhanced the USG's HNPA mission.[189]

---

[186] Cockell, "Civil-Military Responses to Security Challenges in Peace Operations: Ten Lessons from Kosovo," 485. "Foreign Assistance," in *Report to Congressional Requesters* (Washington, DC: GAO, 1993), 1,3.

[187] According to Susan Rice, a permanent U.S. Representative to the United Nations, the U.S. needs the United Nations because it allows the international community to share the cost of operations, provides legitimacy and support through Security Council mandates, and the UN "plays an indispensible role in advancing [U.S.] interests and defending [U.S.]values."(pg 150) In addition, according to a Stimson Center Report, the UN faces many of the same planning, programmatic and operational challenges as the US in HNPA missions but it continues to refine its practices. In Kosovo in particular, the UN led the HNPA mission. Although initially ICITAP planned the mission, it was transferred to UNMIK. The US served as a force and resource provider for UNMIK, but not the command and control element. Both the U.S. and the UN can continue to improve the execution of HNPA missions and must work collectively to institutionalize and support future missions

[188] Richard Swengros, "Military Police Functions in Kosovo," CALL, https://call2.army.mil/rfi/attachments/rfi30983/MP%20Functions%20in%20Kosovo.pdf; Cockell, "Civil-Military Responses to Security Challenges in Peace Operations: Ten Lessons from Kosovo," 484.

[189] ———, "Civil-Military Responses to Security Challenges in Peace Operations: Ten Lessons from Kosovo," 484-85; Bill Piersol et al., "Kosovo Case Study-First 18 Months: March 1999 to September 2000," CALL, https://call2.army.mil/rfi/attachments/rfi30983/Kosovo_Case_Study_199903_20009.pdf.

Objectives provide the motivation and control for subordinates; however, planners must periodically measure and assess them to ensure the continued feasibility and suitability of the plan.[190] Although the endstate remained ill defined, the UN finally developed the Kosovo Standards Implementation Plan and adopted standards for the Kosovars to achieve. Therefore, the international community could periodically assess the progress of UNMIK efforts, and provide resources and support accordingly.[191] The subjective nature of many facets of such missions makes measuring long-term success a challenge; nevertheless, the international community strove to monitor efforts and in turn adjusted the plan accordingly, in order to help Kosovo realize its independence.[192] Both the USG's and the UN's plans required continual scrutiny, reevaluating objectives to identify levels of effectiveness and determine worthiness for funding and resources.[193] As such, in this instance, the components of the performance control method served as constraints limiting the initial success of the KFOR and UNMIK missions.

The budget represents the funding and the resourcing of a mission. Although both KFOR and the UN in Kosovo received adequate funds and equipment, they often suffered from significant staffing shortfalls.[194] The delayed integration of police mentors and security experts meant that the military balanced both the peacekeeping mission and the HNPA mission. Although the DOD may have the capacity, the soldiers, to include the military police, lacked the specific

---

[190] Mintzberg, *The Rise and Fall of Strategic Planning*: 71.

[191] Woehrel and Kim, "Kosovo and US Policy"; Victor Yves Ghebali, "The OSCE norms and activities related to the Security Sector Reform: An incomplete puzzle," *Security and Human Rights* 4(2008): 278,82. The greater the success of the mission the greater the resource allocation for the overall mission.

[192] Yochelson, "The International Criminal Investigative Training Assistance Program".

[193] Andreas Heinemann-Gruder and Igor Grebenschikov, "Security Governance by Internationals: The Case of Kosovo," *International Peacekeeping* 13, no. 1 (March 2006): 48-49.

[194]"Observations on Post-Conflict Assistance in Bosnia, Kosovo, and Afghanistan," in *Testimony* (Washington, DC: GAO, 2003), 7-8. Hansen 104

skills and experience required to establish an effective security apparatus.[195] The delayed

integration of DOJ personnel with the appropriate expertise further hindered the overall mission,

limiting executive leader development and institutional development necessary to sustain the

KPS. The KFOR mission also suffered from additional personnel shortfalls including interpreters,

intelligence personnel, civil affairs advisors, and psychological operations teams, all of whom

could have helped to shape the operation, enhance the flexibility of the commander's response,

and enhanced the HNPA mission.[196]

In addition to personnel, funding also required a significant commitment by the

international community. Funding requirements may not align well with traditional methods of

budgeting. Annual budget cycles and political stipulations negatively affected HNPA missions.

Such missions require a flexible and unique means of resourcing for each mission.[197] Finally,

disparate lines of funding due to the disjointed command and control of the HNPA mission also

affected HNPA missions negatively.[198] Thus limited funding, ill-defined objectives, and the lack

of integrated planning resulted in redundant efforts and inefficiencies during the initial phases of

HNPA in Kosovo. Planners must establish not only the objectives but also the budget and

resources requirements to institute an effective HNPA mission early in the planning effort.

Strategy should guide the establishment of programs and the overarching approach to an

HNPA mission. In Kosovo, the strategy amounted merely to a broad concept facilitating the

---

[195] Swengros, "Military Police Functions in Kosovo"; Jayamaha et al., *Lessons Learned From U.S. Government Law Enforcement In International Operations*: 110; "USAREUR's Army Service Component Command Responsibilities ", CALL, https://call2.army.mil/rfi/attachments/rfi30983/Section%20III%20from%20Joint%20Guardian%20AAR%20Oct%202000.pdf. Military Police are well suited for HNPA at the tactical level but are not trained or equipped to provide institutional or ministerial support.

[196] Swengros, "Military Police Functions in Kosovo".

[197] Cockell, "Civil-Military Responses to Security Challenges in Peace Operations: Ten Lessons from Kosovo," 499; Jayamaha et al., *Lessons Learned From U.S. Government Law Enforcement In International Operations*: 121.

[198] ———, *Lessons Learned From U.S. Government Law Enforcement In International Operations*: 121; Jones et al., "Establishing Law and Order After Conflict".

establishment of ROL, prioritizing the synchronized and integrated development of police, justice, and prison systems that are legitimate in both the eyes of the people and the international community. The Kosovars supported the strategy, which the planners tailored to the context of the situation and culture of the region. Although the UN and the USG conducted limited prior planning, UNMIK eventually developed a comprehensive, two-prong system that included a means of assessment. The plan directed the military to provide emergent security and stability, while over time agencies such as ICITAP, CIVPOL, and UNMIK facilitated a long-term developmental approach for the establishment of the security forces and the necessary institutions for Kosovo. Unfortunately, it not only took time to develop these strategies; it also took time to disseminate, coordinate, and implement the plans, resulting in prolonged insecurity and instability.[199] Finally, the mission lacked the integration of police mentors as part of the initial entry force. Therefore, the lack of integrated planning and the strategies denoted here delayed the success of the HNPA mission in Kosovo.[200]

To counter the ill-defined objectives KFOR and UNMIK worked to develop their own independent strategies. This resulted in gaps, inconsistencies, and poor standardization among all the involved parties.[201] In time, the headquarters conducted limited integrated planning; however, the organizations continued to struggle with the coordination of resources and often failed to apply lessons learned from past HNPA missions.[202] Within the USG's efforts, the DOS developed the policies and strategies instituted by all U.S. forces, while the DOD provided the forces to facilitate such a large and diverse mission. However, this left a gap in expertise. Therefore, to

---

[199] Perito, "U.S. Police in Peace and Stability Operations". Annika Hansen, *From Congo to Kosovo: Civilian Police in Peace Operations* (New York, NY: Oxford University Press, 2002), 104-08.

[200] Jayamaha et al., *Lessons Learned From U.S. Government Law Enforcement In International Operations*: 101; James Brown, "Civil Distrubance: Lessons Learned from Kosovo," *Military Police* (2003): 27-30.

[201] Jayamaha et al., *Lessons Learned From U.S. Government Law Enforcement In International Operations*: 101, 40; "Observations on Post-Conflict Assistance in Bosnia, Kosovo, and Afghanistan," 7.

[202] Jones et al., "Establishing Law and Order After Conflict".

execute its own strategy, the USG resorted to contractors, which resulted in delayed integration, inconsistencies in program implementation, and higher costs.[203] Thus, the strategy and programs – while comprehensive – lacked a level of feasibility and sustainability in Kosovo.

Organizations develop programs in order to implement the strategy. KFOR's initial programs focused on the demilitarization and transformation of the Kosovo Army.[204] Supporting programs included the security and stability of the region by Military Police. The MPs also served as trainers and mentors of the fledgling KPS. With time, the programs evolved. ICITAP focused on institutional processes such as education, management, and ministerial support.[205] Unfortunately, in Kosovo the number of agencies and nations involved in program development and execution led to disjointed, poorly synchronized, and often redundant efforts. To achieve success, program management requires coordination by a lead agency as well as resources, funding, doctrine, and standards. This ensures unity of effort so that all organizations present the same material and methods in support of the HNPA mission.[206] As the mission evolved, KFOR and UNMIK synchronized their efforts and revised the strategy and programs, facilitating the establishment of an effective and respected KPS, as part of the overall security triad.

Although experts consider Kosovo a successful example of SSR and HNPA execution, the mission suffered from many of the same challenges found in both Panama and Haiti. UNMIK, in full partnership with KFOR and the Kosovars, did not establish the Kosovo Standards Implementation Plan until 2005, six years after the enactment of Resolution 1244. This plan serves as an example of detailed integrated planning, linking performance controls to action

---

[203] Jayamaha et al., *Lessons Learned From U.S. Government Law Enforcement In International Operations*: 91.

[204] Heinemann-Gruder and Grebenschikov, "Security Governance by Internationals: The Case of Kosovo," 55.

[205] Jayamaha et al., *Lessons Learned From U.S. Government Law Enforcement In International Operations*: 115-16,18.

[206] Ibid., 119, 42; Piersol et al., "Kosovo Case Study-First 18 Months: March 1999 to September 2000".

planning, strategy and tactics, and all of the efforts of the international community. It defined

standards and objectives and it required consistent assessments in order to alter the plan as

needed. The Kosovo Standards Implementation Plan helped to improve resourcing and

standardization, while empowering the HN to sustain its own security and national

development.[207] KFOR proved that in order to fully realize and implement an effective strategy,

the organizations involved "required a shift in the civilian and military interaction, toward an

integrated planning and shared operations, with all the compromises implicit in the loss of

autonomy."[208] Thus, integrated planning, conducted in full partnership with the HN, collectively

led to the success of the HNPA mission in Kosovo.[209]

Conclusion

The assessment of Operation Promote Liberty in Panama, 1989-1990; Operation Uphold

Democracy in Haiti, 1995-2000; and Kosovo Forces (KFOR) and the United Nations Interim

Administration Mission in Kosovo (UNMIK), 1999-Present in terms of Mintzberg's four

hierarchies (objectives, budgets, strategy, and programs) highlights the strengths and weaknesses

of the USG's efforts in these HNPA missions. The case studies also illustrate the use and

influence of integrated planning methods within HNPA missions. Finally, a synthesis of the case

studies supports recommendations to improve not only the planning process and the execution of

HNPA missions by the USG as a whole but also by the United States Army Military Police

Corps.

---

[207] Woehrel and Kim, "Kosovo and US Policy".

[208] Cockell, "Civil-Military Responses to Security Challenges in Peace Operations: Ten Lessons from Kosovo," 484; "Observations on Post-Conflict Assistance in Bosnia, Kosovo, and Afghanistan," 55-56,60.

[209] Piersol et al., "Kosovo Case Study-First 18 Months: March 1999 to September 2000"; Heinemann-Gruder and Grebenschikov, "Security Governance by Internationals: The Case of Kosovo," 48,55.

Analysis of the case studies demonstrates more integrated planning leads to more effective HNPA efforts in the long term.[210] Integrated planning unifies performance controls and action planning and bridges the gap between general concepts and tangible actions, but this integration takes a concerted effort and appropriate mechanisms.[211] Although not all HNPA missions achieved success, those that did reflected a high level of integrated planning, For example, the USG executed successful HNPA in both Panama and Kosovo. In Panama, the plan evolved after an FBI assessment, while in Kosovo, the Kosovo Standards Implementation Plan led to the successful development of the KPS. However, in Haiti, ICITAP and the UN fostered a five-year plan for the HNP that failed to develop into a successful HNPA mission. Thus, even when planners institute an integrated plan, they must also incorporate a holistic approach addressing the security triad, participation of the HN, and a long-term commitment in order to foster a successful HNPA mission. Therefore, HNPA missions require a balanced approach, detailed long-term planning, commitment, and participation from both the international community and the HN.

Examining the case studies through the lens of the performance control and action planning hierarchies Mintzberg defines in *The Rise and Fall of Strategic Planning* provides a consistent basis for comparison and analysis. (See Appendix B) As discussed, the initial mission set for the military forces did not include HNPA in any of the case studies; therefore, it took time to integrate all of the agencies, resources, and efforts, in order to develop and implement a holistic approach.[212] As a result, the American military consistently provided the stability and security for the HN and in turn conducted the initial assessment, planning, and execution of the

---

[210] Mintzberg, *The Rise and Fall of Strategic Planning*: 67-78.

[211] Ibid., 79-81.

[212] Jayamaha et al., *Lessons Learned From U.S. Government Law Enforcement In International Operations*: 153.

HNPA mission.[213] The lack of planning and preparation for this mission resulted in poorly defined objectives, limited resources, and poorly synchronized strategies and programs, ultimately delaying stability, security, and effective HNPA efforts.[214]

Performance controls are comprised of objectives and budgetary issues. In all three case studies, DOD failed to anticipate a role in HNPA. Therefore, the mission consistently suffered from poor planning, and the lack of comprehensive objectives or adequate resources. The case studies, especially Panama and Kosovo, also reflect the utility of continual assessment and adjustment of the objectives and the HNPA plan. The broad objectives paired with the inconsistent nature of funding and the lack of available assets to conduct HNPA delayed effective and efficient execution of HNPA missions, as illustrated by the delay in the success of the Kosovo mission and the overall failure in Haiti.[215] Even though planners must establish objectives and budgets early on, budgets require a long-term commitment in funding and resources. Planners must tie these elements to the plan and not the results, as demonstrated by the limitation of both funding and resources in Haiti as the mission waned. Finally, The USG or the UN must prepare and stage resources for immediate integration into military operations or deploy them as an independent element before potential mission failure. The delay in non-military resources not only forces the military to fill the gap but also allows instability to fester, reducing military forces' effectiveness as they retrain units for nontraditional missions, and increasing the difficulty of HNPA missions, as seen in all three case studies. Thus, performance controls require

---

[213] Joshua Smith, Victoria Holt, and William Durch, "Enhancing United Nations Capacity to Support Post-Conflict Policing and Rule of Law," The Henry L Stimson Center, http://www.stimson.org/books-reports/enhancing-united-nations-capacity-to-support-post-conflict-policing-and-rule-of-law/.

[214] "Civil Power in Irregular Conflict"; ———, "Enhancing United Nations Capacity to Support Post-Conflict Policing and Rule of Law".

[215] Johnson, Smith, and Farmen, "Mechanics of Governance Approach to Capacity Development," 33-35, 37.

forethought and careful planning as well as long-term support and commitment in order to effectively shape and not simply constrain HNPA missions.

The mission benefits from the integration and balance of performance control and action planning methods. Action planning, unlike performance control methods, leads to the development of strategies and programs through creativity and innovation. Strategy serves as a guide for the execution of HNPA. It requires collaboration between the HN and the agencies and organizations conducting HNPA. The failure in Haiti demonstrates the inability of the UN to understand the operational environment and cultural context of the situation. Additionally, in this example, the HN failed to collaborate with and provide its full support to the forces conducting the HNPA mission. While strategy supports the objectives, programs actually accomplish the mission. Training, mentorship, and institutional development programs are as critical to HNPA as a holist strategic approach that addresses the establishment of ROL, prioritizing the synchronized and integrated development of police, justice, and prison systems that are legitimate in both the eyes of the people and the international community. Panama's success illustrates this point, while the delayed response in Kosovo and the failure of the HNPA mission in Haiti reflect the challenge of synchronizing, facilitating, and supporting comprehensive programs for extended periods. Finally, both strategy and programs benefit from consistent assessments. All three case studies benefitted from internal reviews and periodic assessments that guided the adjustment and execution of the HNPA mission.[216] Therefore, HNPA missions require integrated planning or the successful pairing of performance control and action planning methods, which can bridge the

---

[216] Michelle Hughes, "The Relationship Between SSR and DDR: Impediments to Comprehensive Planning in Military Operations," in *Monopoly of Force: The Nexus of DDR and SSR*, ed. Melanne Civic and Michael Miklaucic (Washington, DC: National Defense University Press, 2011), 242.

great divide and bring together all USG agencies while synchronizing efforts and results in a detailed, holistic approach.[217]

Regardless of the results achieved during SSR and HNPA missions, the efforts illustrated throughout the case studies serve as an example for future engagements. The three case studies exemplify the challenges the USG faces before and during the execution of HNPA missions. For example, HNPA advisors and practitioners consider Panama and Kosovo examples of successful SSR and HNPA missions, yet the overall execution of such missions demonstrates the need for significant reforms.

To improve upon the success of the both Panama and Kosovo HNPA missions, the USG must implement reforms targeting leadership, authorities, and funding and the USG must identify a lead agency. Without a lead agency, efforts will remain redundant and poorly coordinated. Lead agencies not only facilitate integrated planning but also capture lessons learned and establish institutional knowledge in order to prepare for and execute future SSR and HNPA missions effectively. Additionally, a lead agency promotes standardization generating doctrine, common lexicon, and institutional knowledge that enhances HNPA missions.[218] Finally, a lead agency within the USG could provide timely and well-defined objectives and properly coordinated budgetary and resource support. All three case studies clearly demonstrate the impact of delayed preparation and integration of HNPA into the mission set. A lead agency generates unity of effort and serves a proponent for additional programmatic and operational reforms, improving the execution and support of SSR and HNPA missions at large.

---

[217] Jayamaha et al., *Lessons Learned From U.S. Government Law Enforcement In International Operations*: 147, 53; Nguyen, "Swords and Plowshares: DOD and USAID on the Battlefield," 9-10.

[218] An example of a lead agency with the appropriate authorities and resources is the Australian Federal Police International Deployment Group. Glaser. Hughes, "The Relationship Between SSR and DDR: Impediments to Comprehensive Planning in Military Operations," 39,230; Canby, "Roles, Missions, and JTFs: Unintended Consequences," 69.

The USG, after establishing a lead agency, must also redefine and reestablish authorities

for the training and mentorship of foreign police. Proper authorities, superseding FAA, Section

660, which Congress rescinded in 1974, would improve the planning, execution, and assessment

of HNPA missions, provide appropriate leadership, and ensure consistent funding and resourcing

are available.[219]

Lastly, the USG must review the means by which it evaluates the environmental context

and HN partnership before initiating SSR and HNPA missions. Such missions may not succeed if

the HN is unable or unwilling to participate, change, and sustain the strategies and programs.

Thus, the USG must study not only historic cases but also current programmatic challenges and

poor operational systems in order to determine the specific reforms required to improve its

execution of SSR and HNPA.[220]

Although the USG can take several steps to improve the preparation and execution of

SSR, especially HNPA missions, the remainder of this section will focus on what the DOD,

specifically the United States Army Military Police Corps can do to improve its preparation to

support future HNPA missions.[221] Each case study demonstrated the value of the MP Corps as an

---

[219] Ladwig, "Training Foreign Police: A Missing Aspect of U.S Security Assistance to Counterinsurgency," 285; Smith, Holt, and Durch, "Enhancing United Nations Capacity to Support Post-Conflict Policing and Rule of Law"; Dr Corbin Lyday and Jan Stromsem, "Rebuilding the Rule of Law in Post-Conflict Environments," www.usaid.com; "U.S. Security".

[220] "White Paper: Determining the Roles for General Purpose Forces and Special Operations Forces in Security Force Assistance Missions and Refining a Process for Identifying the Best Force for Specific SFA Missions," 6, 8; These issues are addressed and defined in the Argument portion of this monograph on page XX.Bayley, *Changing the Guard: Developing Democratic Police Abroad*: 127.

[221] In addition to revised doctrine, assisting MP's in the planning, preparation and execution of HNPA, the MP Corps now clearly emphasizes ROL and SO in the Regimental Mission and Vision. To improve upon its execution of HNPA, OPMG and USAMPS are focusing on strengthening training programs, increasing exchange opportunities, and beginning to work more closely with the other department-level agencies. Finally, in light of the expansion of the Security Force Assistance Team training mission and the development of the MP Corps plan to support the Army of 2020, the Regiment's Senior Leaders are conducting a capability portfolio review and building on lessons learned from Iraq and Afghanistan. These steps reflect the MP Corps commitment to improving partnership and the overall development of HNPA. U.S. Army, "ATTP 3-39.10 (FM 19-10), Law and Order Operations," Intro, Chapter 7; Fitzgerald and Brady, "Considerations for the Employment of Transitional Law Enforcement

asset in the conduct of HNPA. MP soldiers served as a stopgap, initiating HNPA on behalf of the

DOD and the USG as a whole. While the USG should not rely on soldiers, even MPs, to serve as

the optimal facilitators of HNPA, they have repeatedly demonstrated their ability to take the lead

in the initial phase of HNPA missions.[222] Therefore, the MP Corps can and must continue to

anticipate service in this capacity, and seek to improve not only its preparation for and execution

of HNPA but also its partnership with and transition of HNPA to other USG agencies.[223]

As a branch, the MP Corps should serve as the proponent for the HNPA mission within

DOD. The mission requires both leadership and planning support. Although the DOS will

continue to lead SSR, the DOD must remain prepared to support the initial implementation of the

HNPA mission.[224] The MP Corps can make changes at the strategic and tactical levels to improve

its ability to support HNPA. Primarily, the MP Corps must serve as the U.S. Army's proponent

for HNPA and lead the integrated planning process for HNPA within DOD, bringing all agencies

together and working toward overarching reforms. The approval and publication of *Army Tactics,

Techniques, and Procedures (ATTP) 3-39.10 (FM 19-10) Law and Order Operations*, represents

a crucial first step in assuming this lead role. This manual addresses the HNPA mission,

providing tasks, assessment criteria, and planning considerations. It also provides MP leaders

with a basis to start from, for the planning, preparing, and initial execution of HNPA.[225]

Capabilities"; "Military Police Corps Regiment," (Fort Leonardwood: United States Army Military Police School, 2012).

[222] Martin, "Training Indigenous Security Forces at the Upper End of the Counterinsurgency Spectrum," 61; Bayley and Perito, *The Police in War: Sighting Insurgency, Terrorism, and Violent Crime*: 81, 157; Perito, *Where is the Lone Ranger When We Need Him? America's Search for a Postconflict Stability Force*: 81,85.

[223] Fitzgerald and Brady, "Considerations for the Employment of Transitional Law Enforcement Capabilities".

[224] In order for MPs to participate in Phase 0 operations under the supervision of DOS, it would require expanding authorities for the branch; however, this partnership would allow for skill development, building greater depth of experience, and professional knowledge, subsequently improving the MPs to participation in Phase III-V planning and execution (ultimately improving smoother transitions between each phase).Glaser.

[225] U.S. Army, "ATTP 3-39.10 (FM 19-10), Law and Order Operations," Chapter 7.

As the MP Corps renews its emphasis on L&O operations and ROL, the Provost Marshal General could seek to establish a Joint Interagency Task Force (JIATF) or Joint Interagency Coordination Group (JIACG). Such an organization could provide unity of effort, establish priorities, assign responsibilities, and coordinate resources, greatly enhancing the initial execution of HNPA. A JIATF or a JIACG would enhance unity of effort and open lines of communication between USG agencies, and provide institutional knowledge-to include doctrine, a common lexicon, and a depository for lessons learned. Finally, a JIATF or JIACG would facilitate integrated planning. The military routinely conducts both performance control and action planning methods, but by working with all department-level agencies involved in SSR and HNPA, a JIATF or JIACG dedicated to HNPA could oversee more comprehensive and detailed planning.[226] JIATF or JIACG integrated planning would also ensure the identification of dedicated personnel to initiate HNPA at the onset of military options, properly defined and resourced, thus avoiding the delays that hindered HNPA efforts in Panama, Haiti, and Kosovo. By integrating both military and civilian members, the JIATF or JIACG would greatly enhance the initiation and execution of HNPA.[227]

The MP Corps, through internal reorganization, utilization of all personnel, and increased emphasis on traditional MP missions could improve its HNPA support at both the theater-strategic, operational, and tactical levels. The MP Corps must optimize the utilization of all assets assigned throughout the United States Army, especially staff sections and Table of Organization and Equipment (TOE) units.

---

[226] Schwarzenberg, "Where are the JIACGs Today," 25, 30.

[227] JIATF or JIACG members should include (at a minimum): MP SAMS Planners, Military Intelligence officers, Civil Affairs Officers, Military Information Support Operations Officers and Judge Advocate General Officers, in addition to department-level agencies representatives from DOS-INL, S/CRS, USAID and DOJ-ICITAP and OPDAT. Yeatman, "JIATF-South: Blueprint for Success," 26-27; Canby, "Roles, Missions, and JTFs: Unintended Consequences," 69.

At the theater-strategic level, the Provost Marshal's Office (PMO) in each Unified

Combatant Command (UCC) must take an active role in planning for HNPA missions within its

area of responsibility (AOR). These billets enable the UCCs to identify and understand the

cultural context of the operational environment and unique police and security force structures

and systems, key leaders, and traditional policing methods throughout the respective AORs. The

PM cells, in cooperation with the regionally aligned units, internment and resettlement specialists,

and criminal investigations command agents can synchronize data and their efforts with the

USEMB Team and other organizations like USAID. The PM cells could also foster ROL Teams

within the UCCs, serving as a smaller integrated planning cell, focused on ROL, SSR, and HNPA

mission planning and requirements. By assuming a greater role within the UCC, the PM Cells

augmented by regionally aligned units and MP specialists could foster a greater understanding of

the cultural context of a situation, of the security forces, ultimately improving the planning,

preparation, and execution of HNPA and the integration of the department-level agencies and the

HN.

Additionally, at the strategic and operational level, the DOD should task the U.S. MP

Corps, including the U.S. Army Military Police School, MP Brigade Headquarters, and Criminal

Investigation Division (CID) Group Headquarters to prepare for and support HNPA missions. In

some cases, depending on an individual's background and experience personnel providing

support to HNPA missions, lack the ability to advise and mentor HN Police at the highest levels

and throughout the institutional and sustainment systems.[228] However, by utilizing specific staffs,

and providing them with enhanced training and equipment, the MP Corps would increase the

---

[228] In the past, DOD placed combat arms officers in the lead of HNPA missions, who neither understood the challenges or had the legitamcy in the eyes of the HN, multinational or interaegncy partners to facilitate the mission. Thus, HNPA was not as effective as it could have been. DOD must place senior leaders familiar with the history, and complexity of internantional ROL efforts and the technical aspects of policing as it pertains to SSR. MP Senior leaders are experienced and capable of facilitating HNPA. With increased education, training, and resourcing, the utilization of MPs in HNPA will strengthen the execution and effectiveness of this complex mission. Glaser.

60

range of mentorship that DOD could provide. DoD must place senior leaders familiar with the history, and complecity of interantional RoL efforts and the technical aspects of Policing as it pertains to SSR.

Meanwhile, at the tactical level, the MP Corps must emphasize and support the manning and training of its units down to the individual soldier level. Corps support MP companies possess the capability to execute L&O operations independently; however, due to the current operational tempo of the units, soldiers assigned to billets with additional skill identifiers rarely receive the appropriate corresponding training. Training soldiers to serve as investigators, physical security specialists, and battle staff NCOs would enhance the ability of corps support MP companies to conduct HNPA, including both security and mentorship roles. The MP Corps should consider the integration of CID at the battalion level, just as they integrated 31Es-Correction Specialists at the battalion level to meet operational requirements in Iraq and Afghanistan. The integration of CID personnel would improve the capabilities of an MP battalion and would help strengthen the unit's ability to foster ROL, just as 31Es strengthen their units' ability to mentor HN corrections and investigative personnel.[229] By manning units according to TOE, and integrating all segments of the MP Corps down to the battalion level, MP units would have the required breath of experience for tactical HNPA missions. Thus, fully utilizing and employing organic assets, inherent to the MP Corps would improve DOD's stopgap capabilities and would hasten the planning and execution of HNPA at the strategic and tactical level.

In addition to modifying its personnel management, the MP Corps must better educate its personnel to prepare them to support HNPA missions. While the MP Corps has historically conducted HNPA at the lowest levels, it could broaden the range and depth of experience and

---

[229] Due to CID's unique command and control structure, the MP Corps may need to address and consider the authorities guiding the utilization of agents into non-CID command elements. The MP Corps must therefore develop and provide objectives and intent for their expanded role throughout the MP Branch."U.S. Army Criminal Investigation Command," CID, http://www.cid.army.mil/mission2.html; ibid.

support amongst the branch through additional training, education, assignment to UN missions involving police/ROL capacity building and professionalization efforts and ROL related fellowship opportunities. For example, reestablishing and expanding partnerships with the Federal Law Enforcement Training Center, the FBI, and other agencies including DEA, ATF, and U.S. Marshals in order to expand training opportunities of senior NCOs and officers in specific L&O tasks. So too, would expanding the officer exchange programs with both federal agencies, large police departments across America, and with foreign partners paramilitaries, peacekeeping organizations, and other agencies.[230] Such exchanges would build networks and a working understanding of L&O operations in various types of police structures across the nation. Education and training opportunities not only improve the MP Corps' wealth of experience – they also strengthen ties with department-level agencies and law enforcement experts, all of whom it can call upon for assistance and advice during operational planning and execution. These education, training, and fellowship opportunities benefit both American military police and those of U.S. partners in places worldwide.

In addition to leveraging resources found throughout the law enforcement community, the MP Corps must also develop professional relationships with experts in the academic community. The MP Corps should re-instate the stringent requirements for officers seeking advanced civil schooling opportunities and it should reconsider the type of master's degree associated with the MP Captain's Career Course. By sending officers for degrees specifically focused on elements of criminal justice, the officers would bring back valuable information and foster additional institutional support for HNPA. The MP Corps must focus its efforts to prepare the "force of choice "for this complex and vital mission. The MP Corps has tremendous experience in HNPA missions as illustrated by the case studies described above and from the

---

[230] Partnership and Fellowships could include the United Nations, the Australian Federal Police International Deployment Group, and even agencies such as the United States Institute for Peace and Peacekeeping and Stability Operations Institute.———.

ongoing efforts in Iraq and Afghanistan. It must capture these experiences, using them to instruct the next generation of military police in Pre-Command Courses, mid-grade professional schools and on-line in easily accessible databases for research and review by all members of the profession. The MP Corps must work to lead the DOD in HNPA and to integrate all agencies involved into planning and preparation. By educating the force and improving the knowledge and understanding of HNPA operations, institutions, and expending the network of support, the Corps can prevent the consistent lag in the planning, preparation, and execution of HNPA.

As the wars in Iraq and Afghanistan wind down, the MP Corps must work to maintain and expand on required policing skills, which support the decisive action, while preparing for future engagements. HNPA will remain a reoccurring mission for the USG. [231] Although DOD serves as a supporting element for SSR and HNPA, the MP Corps must work to improve its HNPA capabilities, because history demonstrates it routinely serves as the stopgap and initial response force for HNPA. Taking a practical approach and embracing a frequent, although non-traditional branch mission by proactively cultivating relationships with sister services, department-level agencies and multinational partners (military and civilian), the MP Corps could facilitate improved cooperation, preparation, and execution of HNPA.

Not only must the MP Corps and DOD undergo a cultural transformation, accepting their role in SSR, especially HNPA missions, so too must the other department-level agencies. The USG must embrace the reality and importance of HNPA missions, and in turn resource and empower a lead agency and all supporting agencies. The USG must conduct further analysis of the after action reviews and other analyses of past HNPA missions (as part of the security triad) to improve the nation's ability to conduct SSR, especially HNPA, and consider other alternatives for national-level oversight of these missions. For example, the USG lacks a constabulary or a

---

[231] Gates, "Helping Others Defend Themselves"; Defense, "Sustaining U.S. Global Leadership: Priorities for 21st Century Defense"; Army US, "ADP 3-0 Unified Land Operations," (Washington, DC: Headquarters, Department of the Army, October 2011), iii.

rapidly deployable response force at the federal level (i.e. Australian Federal Police International Deployment Group). A force like this would enable consistent execution of HNPA tasks, improve the USG's response time, decrease the DOD's burden, and mitigate the need for costly contractor support.[232]

The USG should also consider increasing its involvement with international organizations like the UN and CIVPOL. While the United States provides significant financial support to the UN and CIVPOL, it provides limited personnel support. The USG and the international community must establish a more robust partnership in order to capture lessons learned and share experiences.[233]

Another possible course of action would involve the U.S. Army Military Police Corps assuming a radical shift in mission and authorities, in order to serve as the national constabulary, tailored to conduct HNPA mission support. This would drastically alter the mission focus, TOE, personnel policies, and doctrine of the MP Corps, but it would provide greater flexibility for the USG if given the authority required to execute HNPA fully.[234] Although not a new mission, HNPA as a subset of SSR continues to grow in importance and by integrating the elements of national power and by implementing reforms the USG could improve its execution of HNPA. Therefore, preventing failing states from failing and re-establishing failed states, improving security worldwide.

---

[232] Perito, *Where is the Lone Ranger When We Need Him? America's Search for a Postconflict Stability Force*: 5-6, 33.

[233] Susan Rice, "Why America Needs the UN: Six Reasons the United Nations is Indispensable," McMurry, Inc, www.vsotd.com; William Durch, "United Nations Police Evolution, Present Capacity, and Future Tasks," The Henry L Stimson Center, http://www.stimson.org/research-pages/police-building-united-nations-police-evolution-present-capacity-and-future-tasks/.

[234] If the MP Corps assumes the mission of a constabulary force, the Regiment should seek the authority to allow for lateral entry into the organization, similar to what the medical service branch does for doctors, in order to seek out high end skills and experience sets and bring them into the organization Glaser.

The DOD, DOS, and DOJ must improve their collaboration to develop tactics, techniques, and procedures required to facilitate effective SSR and HNPA, which require a tremendous amount of reform at all levels to establish an effective and efficient means to facilitate the mission. To develop true effectiveness, these agencies must 1) improve their planning for HNPA missions, 2) implement programmatic changes addressing, in particular, authorities, lines of funding, and manning and 3) revise the operational systems utilized, like means of assessment, training, and implementation methods to achieve greater long term success. The USG should not simply use SSR, SFA, and HNPA as a means of post-conflict intervention. These missions also foster security, stability, and most importantly "'Liberty [which] begins with the protection of life secured by law....'"[235] Thus, HNPA warrants careful study and continued reform. These missions possess utility for intervention in failing states, to prevent the collapse of security and the loss of a government's ability to protect and provide for its citizens, generating stability, allowing legitimacy to flourish, and improving global security, all while promoting and safeguarding American democratic ideals.

---

[235] "Host Nation Policing Advising Training Support Package: Police Advising Overview," slide 2.

Appendix A

Acronyms

AOR	Area of Responsibility
ATTP	Army Tactics, Techniques, and Procedures
CIVPOL	Civilian Police International
CMOC	Civil Military Operations Center
CRS	Congressional Research Service
DOD	Department of Defense
DOJ	Department of Justice
DOS	Department of State
FAA	Foreign Assistance Act
FBI	Federal Bureau of Investigations
GAO	Government Accountability Office
HN	Host Nation
HNP	Haitian National Police
HNPA	Host Nation Police Advisory
ICITAP	International Criminal Investigative Training Advisory Program
INL	Bureau of International Narcotics and Law Enforcement Affairs
IPM	International Police Monitor
IPSF	Interim Public Security Force
JIACG	Joint Interagency Coordination Group
JIATF	Joint Interagency Task Force
KFOR	Kosovo Forces
KPS	Kosovo Police Services
L&O	Law and Order Operations
LTG	Lieutenant General

MAT	Military Assistance Team.
MNF	Multinational Force
MP	Military Police
MSG	Military Support Group
NATO	North Atlantic Treaty Organization
OPDAT	Office of Overseas Prosecutorial Development, Assistance, and Training
OPLAN	Operation Plan
OPS	Office of Public Safety
OSCE	Organization for Security and Co-operation in Europe
PDF	Panamanian Defense Force
PKSOI	Peacekeeping and Stability Operations Institute
PMO	Provost Marshal Office
PNP	Panamanian National Police
RAND	Research and Development
ROL	Rule of Law
S/CRS	Office of the Coordinator for Reconstruction and Stabilization[236]
SFA	Security Force Assistance
SO	Stability Operations
SSR	Security Sector Reform
TOE	Table of Organization and Equipment
UCC	Unified Combatant Command
UN	United Nations
UNMIK	United Nations Interim Administration Mission in Kosovo

---

[236] Department of State will integrate S/CRS into the Bureau of Conflict and Stabilization Operations after January 2012. "Bureau of Conflict and Stabilization Operations".

USAID	U.S. Agency for International Development
USAMPS	U.S. Army Military Police School
USEMB	U.S. Embassy
USG	United States Government

Appendix B

	Panama 1989-1990	Haiti 1995-2000	Kosovo 1999-Present
Participants	Unilateral: USG agencies	Multilateral: UN/U.S.	Multilateral: UN/U.S.
Planning Process	Transitioned to integrated planning after ICITAP established as lead agency	Limited integration-unable to collaborate with GoH	Became integrated after 2005
Objectives SSR/HNPA an after thought; often broad and ill-defined	Ill-defined Security-democratization-transition to GoP	Defined by Governor's Island Agreement; however, lacked objectives by phase or true integration of GoH; security and stability-transition to UN (rushed-unrealistic timeline)	Defined by UN Resolution 1244 and follow-on mandates; no endstate identified; security and stability
Budget Mission exceeds initial timeline/resource intensive	Financially sound; limited personnel/ICITAP unprepared and under strength	Budget based on success-robust initially, waned when progress slowed, based on 6 mo mandates; GoH unable to sustain	Budget based on success-robust initially, waned when progress slowed; Inconsistent funding, limited commitment of personnel
Strategy Suffers from ill-defined Obj./Military CAP institutes ad hoc strategy	Delayed-ad hoc-military led; Transition from PDF to PNP through MSG, ICITAP, Triad approach	Transition from Military to IPSF to HNP; Unbalanced Triad; Transition to UN –poor coordination/buy-in from GoH	Development of KPS; triad-initially unbalanced; strategy not linked to resources— stunted by ill-defined obj; lack HN integration and buy-in
Programs Often redundant and poorly coordinated; lacks assessment and standardization	2 TNG programs; Emergent and PNP; Partnership and Mentorship-MPs and ICITAP collective; Guns for Money and Tips Hotline	Integrate IPM and MATs, MP support. Training and Mentorship through MPs, ICITAP, IPM-academy established	MPs, CIVPOL, limited ICITAP integration-academy established; mentorship, training; redundant efforts-poor coordination
Long Term Plan Demonstrates the evolution and adoption of integrated planning	After FBI Evaluation-Strategy Implemented	HNP only element with long term plan	After 2005 Kosovo Standards Implementation Plan

Table 1: Summary of Case Study Analysis

The Table represents a brief comparison of the three case studies analyzed: Operation Promote Liberty in Panama, 1989-1990; Operation Uphold Democracy in Haiti, 1995-2000; and Kosovo Forces (KFOR) and the United Nations Interim Administration Mission in Kosovo (UNMIK), 1999-Present. The far let column represents Minzberg's hierarchies, which were the bases of comparison for this monograph. The column also represents several elements that affected the planning process and the outcome of each HNPA Mission. This table also reflects trends such as the eventual establishment of integrated planning, the length of the mission and the comprehensive approach targeting the security triad collectively. The data depicted on the chart as well as the details discussed at length in each case study shaped the recommendations for reform and the overall conclusion for this monograph.

Bibliography

"The Army Capstone Concept." US Army TRADOC,
    http://www.tradoc.army.mil/tpubs/pams/tp525-3-0.pdf.

"Assistance for Civilian Policing: USAID Policy Guidance." www.usaid.com.

Baltazar, Thomas, and Elizabeth Kvitashvilli. "The Role of USAID and Development Assistance
    in Combating Terrorism." *Military Review* (March-April 2007): 36-40.

Bayley, David. *Changing the Guard: Developing Democratic Police Abroad.* New York, NY:
    Oxford University Press, 2006.

Bayley, David, and Robert Perito. *The Police in War: Sighting Insurgency, Terrorism, and
    Violent Crime.* Boulder, CO: Lynne Rienner Publishers, Inc, 2010.

Beede, Benjamin. "The Roles of Paramilitary and Militarized Police." *Journal of Political and
    Military Sociology* 36, no. 1 (Summer 2008): 53-63.

Brown, James. "Civil Distrubance: Lessons Learned from Kosovo." *Military Police* (2003).

Bryden, Alan. "The DDR-SSR Nexus." In *Monopoly of Force the Nexus of DDR and SSR*, edited
    by Melanne Civic and Michael Miklaucic, 233-48. Washington, DC: National Defense
    University Press, 2011.

"Bureau of Conflict and Stabilization Operations." U.S. Department of State,
    http://www.state.gov/j/cso/.

"Bureau of International Narcotics and Law Enforcement Affairs." U.S. Department of State,
    http://www.state.gov/g/inl/.

Bushman, John. "Standing Joint Task Forces: Resourcing Relics." United States Army Command
    and General Staff College, AY 2009-2010.

Caldwell, William, and Steven Leonard. "Field Manual 3-07, Stability Operations: Upshifting the
    Engine of Change." *Military Review* (July-August 2008): 2-9.

Canby, Steven. "Roles, Missions, and JTFs: Unintended Consequences." *Joint Forces Quarterly*
    (Autumn/Winter 1994-95): 68-75.

Caslen, Robert. "Change 1 to Field Manual 3-0 the Way the Army Fights Today." *Military
    Review* (March-April 2011): 84-88.

Christoff, Joseph. "Training and Equipping Foreign Police Forces." General Accounting Office,
    www.gao.gov/podcast/watchdog_episode_56.html.

Chura-Beaver, Jacqueline. "Developing Host Nation Law Enforcement Capacity for Security
    Transition." www.PKSOI.army.mil.

"Civil Power in Irregular Conflict." Peacekeeping and Stability Operations Institute, http://pksoi.army.mil/PKM/publications/reports/documents/CNA_PKSOI_civil-power-in-irregular-conflict_all.pdf.

Cockell, John. "Civil-Military Responses to Security Challenges in Peace Operations: Ten Lessons from Kosovo." *Global Governance*, no. 8 (2002): 483-502.

Cole, Beth, ed. *Guiding Principles for Stabilization and Reconstruction.* Washington, DC: USIP Press, 2009.

Cole, Ronald. "Operation Just Cause: The Planning and Execution of Joint Operations in Panama February 1988-January 1990." Washington, DC: Joint History Office, 1995.

Davis, Reg, and Harry James. "The Public Safety Story." In *The Public Safety Newsletter.* Santee, CA, 2001.

Defense, Department of. "Department of Defense Instruction 3000.05." http://www.dtic.mil/whs/directives/corres/pdf/300005p.pdf.

———. "Sustaining U.S. Global Leadership: Priorities for 21st Century Defense." http://www.defense.gov/news/Defense_Strategic_Guidance.pdf.

Deflem, Mathieu. "Global Rule of Law or Global Rule of Law Enforcement? International Police Cooperation and Counter-Terrorism." IOS Press.

Durch, William. "United Nations Police Evolution, Present Capacity, and Future Tasks." The Henry L Stimson Center, http://www.stimson.org/research-pages/police-building-united-nations-police-evolution-present-capacity-and-future-tasks/.

Fitzgerald, Ben, and Scott Brady. "Considerations for the Employment of Transitional Law Enforcement Capabilities." Peacekeeping and Stability Operations Institute, http://pksoi.army.mil/PKM/documents/Noetic%20TLE%20Project%20Considerations%20for%20TLE%20-%20Jan%2009.pdf.

"Foreign Assistance." In *Report to Congressional Requesters.* Washington, DC: GAO, 1993.

"Foreign Assistance Meeting the Training Needs of Police in New Democracies." Government Accountability Office, http://www.gao.gov/products/NSIAD-93-109.

"Foreign Assistance Status of Rule of Law Program Coordinator." US Government Accountability Office, http://pdf.usaid.gov/pdf_docs/PCAAA793.pdf.

Garrett, Kenneth. "In Both Jungle and Urban Operations." *Military Police* (Spring 1992): 40-41.

Gates, Robert. "Helping Others Defend Themselves." http://www.foreignaffairs.com/articles/66224/robert-m-gates/helping-others-defend-themselves.

Gerspacher, Nadia. "The History of International Police Cooperation: A 150-Year Evolution in Trends and Approaches." *Global Crime* 9, no. 1-2 (February-May 2008): 169-84.

Ghebali, Victor Yves. "The OSCE Norms and Activities Related to the Security Sector Reform: An Incomplete Puzzle." *Security and Human Rights* 4 (2008).

Glaser, David. Email correspondence with author. Provided insight and commentary regarding content of monograph, February 9, 2012.

Green, Stephen. "Augmentation Units in Panama." *Military Police* (Spring 1993): 11.

Grigsby, Wayne, Scott Gorman, Jack Marr, Joseph McLamb, Michael Stewart, and Pete Schifferle. "Integrated Planning the Operations Process, Design, and the Military Decision Making Process." *Military Review* (January-February 2011): 28-34.

Gwaltney, Alton. "Law and Order in Kosovo: A Look at Criminal Justice During the First Year of Operation Joint Guardian." The Command and Control Research Program, https://call2.army.mil/rfi/attachments/rfi30983/CCRP_Lessons_from_Kosovo_Wentz_Nov02.pdf.

"Haiti in Extremis." *The Christian Century* (March 1, 2000): 227-28.

Halverson, Ronald, and Paul Bliese. "Determinants of Soldier Support for Operation Uphold Democracy." *Armed Forces & Society* 23, no. 1 (Fall 1996): 81-96.

Hansen, Annika. *From Congo to Kosovo: Civilian Police in Peace Operations*. New York, NY: Oxford University Press, 2002.

Heinemann-Gruder, Andreas, and Igor Grebenschikov. "Security Governance by Internationals: The Case of Kosovo." *International Peacekeeping* 13, no. 1 (March 2006): 43-59.

Ho, Timothy JG. "Ordering Disorder: An Evaluation of the Effectiveness of International Civilian Police Training in Haiti, 1994-2001." Royal Roads University, 2006.

"Host Nation Policing Advising Training Support Package: Police Advising Overview." Fort Leonard Wood, MO: United States Army Military Police School, 2011.

Hughes, Michelle. "The Relationship between SSR and DDR: Impediments to Comprehensive Planning in Military Operations." In *Monopoly of Force: The Nexus of DDR and SSR*, edited by Melanne Civic and Michael Miklaucic, 27-40. Washington, DC: National Defense University Press, 2011.

Hume, Elizabeth, and Michael Miklaucic. "Exorcising Demons of the Past: Seizing New Opportunities to Promote Democratic Policing." In *2005 USAID Summer Seminar Series*: USAID, July 7, 2005.

Hurwitz, Agnes, and Gordon Peake. "Strengthening the Security-Development Nexus: Assessing International Police and Practice since the 1990s." International Peace Academy, www.ipacademy.org.

"ICITAP Strategic Plan Fiscal Years 2009-2013." Department of Justice: Criminal Division, http://www.justice.gov/criminal/icitap/about/strategic-plan.html.

"ICITAP/Panama Police Training Project Evaluation: Final Report." Arlington, VA: National Center for State Courts, August 1994.

" International Criminal Investigative Training Assistance Program." U.S. Department of Justice, http://www.justice.gov/criminal/icitap/.

"International Security: DOD and State Need to Improve Sustainment Planning and Monitoring and Evaluation for Section 1206 and 1207 Assistance Programs." US Government Accountability Office, www.gao.gov/products/GAO-10-431.

Jayamaha, Dilshika, Scott Brady, Ben Fitzgerald, and Jason Fritz. *Lessons Learned from U.S. Government Law Enforcement in International Operations*, PKSOI Papers. Carlisle, PA: Strategic Studies Institute, 2010.

Johnson, Matthew, William Smith, and William Farmen. "Mechanics of Governance Approach to Capacity Development." *InterAgency Journal* 2, no. 2 (Summer 2011): 33-40.

"Joint Interagency Task Force West." http://www.pacom.mil/web/site_pages/staff%20directory/jiatfwest/jiatfwest.shtml.

Jones, Seth, Jeremy Wilson, Andrew Rathmell, and K. Jack Riley. "Establishing Law and Order after Conflict." RAND, http://www.rand.org/pubs/monographs/MG374.html.

Keller, Dennis. "U.S. Military Forces and Police Assistance in Stability Operations: The Least-Worst Option to Fill the U.S. Capacity Gap." http://www.strategicstudiesinstitute.army.mil/.

Kelly, Justin, and Mike Brennan. "Alien: How Operational Art Devoured Strategy." Strategic Studies Institute, http://www.strategicstudiesinstitute.army.mil/pubs/display.cfm?pubID=939.

Ladwig, Walter. "Training Foreign Police: A Missing Aspect of U.S Security Assistance to Counterinsurgency." *Comparative Strategy: An International Journal* 26, no. 4 (July-September 2007): 285-93.

Lafferty, Patrick. "The 511th Mlitary Police Company in Cap Haitian, Haiti." *Military Police* (Winter 1995): 20-24.

Locher, James. "The Most Important Thing: Legislature Reform of the National Security System." *Military Review* (May-June 2008): 4-12.

Lyday, Dr Corbin, and Jan Stromsem. "Rebuilding the Rule of Law in Post-Conflict Environments." www.usaid.com.

Mackey, Robert. "The Triple Threat in Operation Just Cause." *Military Police* (Winter 1990): 6-10.

Marquis, Jefferson P, Jennifer Moroney, Justin Beck, Derek Eaton, Scott Hiromoto, David Howell, Janet Lewis, Charlotte Lynch, Michael Neumann, and Cathryn Thruston. "Developing an Army Strategy for Building Partner Capacity for Stability Operations." RAND Corporation, http://www.rand.org/pubs/monographs/MG942.html.

Martin, John. "Training Indigenous Security Forces at the Upper End of the Counterinsurgency Spectrum." *Military Review* 86, no. 6 (November/December 2006): 58-64.

Maxfield, N. "Uphold Democracy: 503rd MP BN." *Paraglide*, October 6, 1994.

McFate, Sean. "There's a New Sheriff in Town: DDR-SSR and the Monopoly of Force." In *Monopoly of Force the Nexus of DDR and SSR*, edited by Melanne Civic and Michael Miklaucic, 213-32. Washington, DC: National Defense University Press, 2001.

Meharg, Sarah, and Aleisha Arnusch. "Security Sector Reform: A Case Study Approach to Transition and Capacity Building." Strategic Studies Institute, http://www.strategicstudiesinstitute.army.mil/.

Mendelson-Forman, Johanna. "Security Sector Reform in Haiti." *International Peacekeeping* 13, no. 1 (March 2006): 14-27.

"Military Police Corps Regiment." Fort Leonardwood: United States Army Military Police School, 2012.

Mintzberg, Henry. *The Rise and Fall of Strategic Planning*. New York: The Free Press, 1994.

"Multiple U.S. Agencies Provided Billions of Dollars to Train and Equip Foreign Police Forces." US Government Accountability Office, http://www.gao.gov/products/GAO-11-402R.

"National Security Strategy." White House, http://www.whitehouse.gov/sites/default/files/rss_viewer/national_security_strategy.pdf.

Nguyen, Quy. "Swords and Plowshares: DOD and USAID on the Battlefield." *InterAgency Journal* 2, no. 2 (Summer 2011): 8-15.

O'Neill, William. "Police Reform in Post-Conflict Societies: What We Know and What We Still Need to Know." International Peace Academy, www.ipacademy.org.

"Observations on Post-Conflict Assistance in Bosnia, Kosovo, and Afghanistan." In *Testimony*. Washington, DC: GAO, 2003.

"Office of Overseas Prosecutorial Development, Assistance and Training." U.S. Department of Justice, http://www.justice.gov/criminal/opdat/.

"Operation Uphold Democracy: US Forces in Haiti." Norfolk, VA: U.S. Atlantic Command, May 1997.

"Operation Uphold or Something: Haiti (U.S. Military Intervention)." http://www.highbeam.com/doc/1G1-15768453.html.

Patton, David. "Operation Just Cause." Fort Bragg, NC: Provost Marshal Office, 82nd Airborne Division, 1990.

Perito, Robert. "U.S. Police in Peace and Stability Operations." United States Institute of Peace Press, www.usip.org.

————. *Where Is the Lone Ranger When We Need Him? America's Search for a Postconflict Stability Force*. Washington, DC: United States Institute of Peace Press, 2004.

Piersol, Bill, Gary Horne, Ulrike Lechner, and Agatino Mursia. "Kosovo Case Study-First 18 Months: March 1999 to September 2000." CALL, https://call2.army.mil/rfi/attachments/rfi30983/Kosovo_Case_Study_199903_20009.pdf.

Pittman, Garry, and Dan Simpson. "Fighting Crime in Panama." *Military Police* (Spring 1993): 4-7.

"Quadrennial Defense Review." Department of Defense, http://www.defense.gov/qdr/images/QDR_as_of_12Feb10_1000.pdf.

"Quadrennial Diplomacy and Development Review." Department of State, http://www.state.gov/documents/organization/153142.pdf.

Rice, Susan. "Why America Needs the UN: Six Reasons the United Nations Is Indispensable." McMurry, Inc, www.vsotd.com.

Riegg, Nicholas. "Concepts and Systems for States in Crisis." *InterAgency Journal* 1, no. 1 (Fall 2010): 33-40.

Russell, Laura. "Restoring Law and Order." *Military Police* (Spring 1993): 8-12.

Schilling, Anthony. "Law and Order South of the Border." *Military Police* (Winter 1990): 12-15.

Schwarzenberg, Jan. "Where Are the JIACGs Today." *InterAgency Journal* 2, no. 2 (Summer 2011): 24-31.

Serafino, Nina. "Policing in Peacekeeping and Related Stability Operations: Problems and Proposed Solutions." Congressional Research Service, www.fas.org/man/crs/RL32321.pdf

Smith, Joshua, Victoria Holt, and William Durch. "Enhancing United Nations Capacity to Support Post-Conflict Policing and Rule of Law." The Henry L Stimson Center, http://www.stimson.org/books-reports/enhancing-united-nations-capacity-to-support-post-conflict-policing-and-rule-of-law/.

Stahl, David. "Operation Uphold Democracy Operations in Haiti August 1994 Thru January 1995 ". Fort Eustic, VA: Training and Audiovisual Support Center.

Steffan. "Multinational Force Haiti: Operation Uphold Democracy and 10th Mountain Division Operations in Haiti." edited by US Army War College. Center For Army Lessons Learned, February 28, 1995.

Stodiek, Thorsten. "OSCE's Police-Related Activities: Lessons Learned During the Last Decade." *Security and Human Rights*, no. 3 (2009): 201-11.

Strickler, Ted. "What the QDDR Says About Interagency Coordination." *InterAgency Journal* 2, no. 1 (Winter 2011): 67-73.

Stromsem, Janice, and Joseph Trincellito. "Building the Haitian National Police: A Retrospective and Prospective View." The Haiti Program, http://trincellito.com/user/HNPTrinity.final.pdf.

Swengros, Richard. "Military Police Functions in Kosovo." CALL, https://call2.army.mil/rfi/attachments/rfi30983/MP%20Functions%20in%20Kosovo.pdf.

Taw, Jennifer Morrison. "Operation Just Cause: Lessons for Operations Other Than War." Arroyo Center, http://www.rand.org/pubs/monograph_reports/MR569.html.

"U.S. Agency for International Development." U.S. Agency for International Development, http://www.usaid.gov/.

U.S. Army. "ADP 3-0 Unified Land Operations." Washington, DC: Headquarters, Department of the Army, October 2011.

U.S. Army. "ATTP 3-39.10 (FM 19-10), Law and Order Operations." Washington, DC: Headquarters, Department of the Army, June 2011.

———. "Field Manual 3-07, Stability Operations." Washington, DC: Headquarters, Department of the Army, October 2008.

———. "Field Manual 3-07.1, Security Force Assistance." Washington, DC: Headquarters, Department of the Army, May 2009.

———. "FM 1-02: Operational Terms and Graphics." Washington, DC: Headquarters, Department of the Army, September 2004.

———. "FM 5-0 C1: The Operations Process, Change 1." Washington, DC: Headquarters, Department of the Army, March 18, 2011.

"U.S. Army Criminal Investigation Command." CID, http://www.cid.army.mil/mission2.html.

U.S. Department of Justice. "About ICITAP." http://www.justice.gov/criminal/icitap/.

"U.S. Security." Global Security, http://www.globalsecurity.org/intell/library/reports/gao/920300-train.htm.

"United States Army Military Police School." MP Corps, http://www.wood.army.mil/usamps/.

"USAREUR's Army Service Component Command Responsibilities ". CALL, https://call2.army.mil/rfi/attachments/rfi30983/Section%20III%20from%20Joint%20Guardian%20AAR%20Oct%202000.pdf.

"White Paper: Determining the Roles for General Purpose Forces and Special Operations Forces in Security Force Assistance Missions and Refining a Process for Identifying the Best Force for Specific SFA Missions." edited by JCISFA. Ft Leavenworth, KS: JCISFA, June 2008.

Woehrel, Steven J, and Julie Kim. "Kosovo and US Policy." Congressional Research Service, www.fas.org/sgp/crs/row/RL31053.pdf

Yates, Lawrence. "Operation Just Cause in Panama City, December 1989." In *Block by Block: The Challenge of Urban Operations*, edited by William Robertson and Lawrence Yates. Fort Leavenworth, KS: U.S. Army Command and General Staff College Press, 2002.

———. "Panama, 1988-1999: The Disconnect between Combat and Stability Operations." *Military Review* (May-June 2005): 46-52.

Yeatman, Richard. "JIATF-South: Blueprint for Success." *Joint Forces Quarterly*, no. 42 (3rd Quarter 2006): 26-27.

Yochelson, Roger. "The International Criminal Investigative Training Assistance Program." Resource Library: The CBS Interactive Network, findarticles.com/p/articles/mi_m2194/is_n4_v62/ai_13859797.